JEFF HARLOW

Acts 3 Discovery

Participant Guide

Discovering What God Gave You,

Finding the Reasons Why

Also by Jeff Harlow:

Dancing with Cinderella: Leading a Healthy Church Transition

Any vision that underestimates the importance of leadership transition is incomplete. After all, God's purposes have longer shelf lives than His leaders.

Dancing with Cinderella outlines several core principles drawn from Jeff Harlow's leadership transition as the senior pastor of a church of over 3000 members. It serves to help other leaders navigate the organizational, relational, and emotional details of a leadership transition without losing momentum. It doesn't matter if you're the leader of a small or large church, old or plant church, traditional or contemporary church, obscure or iconic church; an unhealthy leadership transition hurts people and cripples mission.

Jeff's story will help a leader, the leadership teams, and the members of a church think through the principles of transition as they prepare for the exit of a current pastor and the entrance of their new leader. In these pages you can discover how to do transition right, so you don't have to figure out why it went wrong.

The Sacred Switch: The Subtle Shift from Grabbing to Giving

After the prepping years of your youth and the building years of early adulthood, what plans does God have for you in the 3rd stage of life?

God has a plan for every season and stage of your life. He knows the plan(s) He has for you, and those plans slowly unfold and compound according to His perfect timing and infinite resourcefulness.

This same pattern is found in the creation of the universe. Rather than lay out all creation in a single instant, He paced Himself and sequentially built upon His work. So He is with His children. He gradually transforms us to be more and more like Christ, and He does so year by year, season by season, and stage by stage, until our final breath – and beyond. From glory to glory.

The Sacred Switch outlines this divine process and your role in it. It illustrates how God, in His perfect timing, will flip a switch deep within you and develop you from one stage of life to the next. And for those entering the 3rd Stage of Life, it will guide you to recognize and appreciate how resilient, mysterious, intricate, and beautiful His plan(s) truly are as you make the subtle shift from grabbing to giving.

Acts 3 Discovery

Participant Guide

*Discovering What God Gave You,
Finding the Reasons Why*

ACT3MINISTRY.COM

Copyright © 2025 by Jeff Harlow
Cover and internal design © 2025 by Epiphany Publishing, LLC
Cover photo is "Peaks of the Dolomites," by derProjektor via Photocase.com.

All rights reserved. No part of this book may be reproduced in any form, stored in a retrieval system, or transmitted in any form by any means (electronic, mechanical, photocopy, recording, or otherwise), without prior permission in writing from the copyright owner, except for the inclusion of a brief quotation in critical articles and reviews.

Published in Indianapolis, Indiana by Epiphany Publishing, LLC.

Unless otherwise indicated, all Scripture quotations are taken from the Holy Bible, New International Version (NIV). © 1973, 1978, 1984 by International Bible Society. Used by permission. All rights reserved worldwide.

Scripture quotations marked NKJV are taken from the New King James Version®. Copyright © 1982 by Thomas Nelson. Used by permission. All rights reserved.

Scriptures marked NASU are taken from the NEW AMERICAN STANDARD UPDATED (NASU): Scripture taken from the NEW AMERICAN STANDARD UPDATED BIBLE®, copyright©, 1995 by The Lockman Foundation. Used by permission.

The *Calling Star*™ symbol is a registered trademark of ACT3 Ministry. All rights reserved.

For information about special discounts available for bulk purchases, sales promotions, fund-raising, and educational needs, contact Epiphany Publishing Sales at sales@epiphanypublishing.us.

Library of Congress Control Number: 2018959390

ISBN 9781946093196
ISBN 9781946093110 (2018 version)

First printing in 2018. November 2025 version.
This book was printed in the United States of America.

Epiphany Publishing
P.O. Box 36814
Indianapolis, IN 46236
www.epiphanypublishing.us
info@epiphanypublishing.us

Contents

Introduction vii
How to Use This Guide ix
Calling Star xiii

Week 1: Regaining Your Bearings 15
Week 2: ReFocusing Your Heart 25
Week 3: ReThinking Your Path 31
Week 4: Exploring the Impact of Your Journey 41
Week 5: Admiring the Master's 1st Stroke 43
Week 6: Celebrating Your Strengths 47
Week 7: Embracing Your Spiritual Gifts 53
    Understanding Spiritual Gifts 61
    Spiritual Gifts Application Guide 65
Week 8: ReCalculating the Value of Relationships and Your Own Worth 81
Week 9: Gauging Your Resources of Time and Talents 89
Week 10: Detecting the Heat of Your Passions 97

Driving a Stake in the Ground 105

Worksheets

    Journey Map Worksheet 107
    Strengths Worksheet 109
    People Worksheet 111
    Passions Worksheet 113
    Skills Worksheet 115
    Time Worksheet 117
    Next Steps Exploration Worksheet 121

About the Authors 125
About the Publisher 127

Introduction

If an eagle that had just caught an updraft for a soar could talk, don't you know it would scream, "*I was made for this!*" If an apple tree loaded with flawless fruit could talk, don't you know it would whisper, "*I was made for this!*" If a child's mind could be read while playing a favorite game with his or her best friends, don't you know the words would shout, "*I was made for this!*"

Do you know what you were made for? Do you know what you are made of which makes that possible? Can you recognize the assignments in this season of your life that are aligned with what Creator God made you for and what He made you of?

Welcome to your Acts 3 Discovery experience. Join Peter in his new day as recorded in Acts 3. He had been born a Simon, but with the potential to be a Peter. We don't know how old he was (because it makes no difference), but it had taken some time and an array of experiences for him to learn who he really was and what he was really made for. Once the lights came on, Peter would never be known as Simon again. He still had his moments, but the experiences recorded in Scripture demanded he live them out as the Peter Jesus promised to make of him. On that normal day on the way to the Temple to pray, he turned the man in the story's life right-side-up, Jerusalem upside-down, and launched the newborn Church in motion for her next steps forward.

It was with you in mind this guide was produced. It was for one purpose this process was developed. At the heart of this study is the hope that you will confirm what makes you the Master's masterpiece and discover opportunities to engage at your fullest potential. Every effort was driven by the urge for you to experience the profound joy of partnering with the King to impact an outcome your world desperately needs. We want your breath to be taken by reflexively thinking, "*I was made for this!*" You can't allow yourself to exhale your last breath bereft of that mountaintop experience.

Our highest hope is that with each lesson and every assessment, the foggy mirror will clear and reflect the beautiful you, the only you God has ever made. It is our deepest desire that with every conversation the lights will brighten the pathway that leads you to your calling and every assignment it entails in every stage of your life. We want to be in the crowd cheering when Jesus embraces you in Heaven and says loudly enough for everyone to hear: *Well done!*

Enjoy rediscovering your calling,
Jeff Harlow

How to Use This Guide

Icons—Explanations of the icons used in this content are listed at the end of this segment.

Participant Information—Contact information for each participant of our group has been included as available. You are also given ample space to jot personal facts that participants share. Getting to know and becoming known is a huge advantage in this Discovery process. You may have a new close friend that you will meet for the first time in this Discovery Cohort.

Group Dialogue—Your experience will be enriched by the conversations that are directed within the times of sharing. Those conversations will take place in three different types of structured environments: At times, the conversations will include the entire group. Some of the discussions will take place in smaller clusters comprised of others at your table or those sitting closest to you. Finally, the deepest sharing will take place in the personal settings of 2-3 participants.

Scripture Study—Your Discovery process is undergirded with Scripture. The confidence you can have in the power of this process is that it is based solidly on scriptural principles and Biblical Truth.

Assessment Tools—A personal strengths assessment will be provided separately. A link to an electronic Spiritual Gifts Assessment will be provided by email during the week it is assigned as homework. A manual version can be supplied upon request. If you have taken a spiritual gifts assessment in the past year, feel free to use those findings. If it has been longer than that, then your time would be well spent to take an assessment again. Your discovery guide will support you for your time study.

Calling Star—Your *Calling Star* (p. xiii) is the composite picture of the masterpiece God has made you to be. A loose-leaf copy is provided in the supplemental folder given to you at the first Cohort gathering. Don't wait until the last minute to distill the information and input it into the appropriate points of the star. Keep it current. Enjoy the process of watching it come together.

Going Deeper — Our meetings are fast-paced and flush with rich content. Time is a factor. Starting on time is imperative. Even then, powerful truths are left for you to personally pursue. When there is more content than time, we supply a section at the end of the chapter entitled Going Deeper. *This is not like extra credit!* It serves to enhance your experience and strengthen your grip on the Discovery process. Though the studies are optional, we believe you will find them invaluable.

Subject Experts — Sometimes you may be given the opportunity of a guest facilitator, particularly trained to facilitate the subject and discussion of the evening.

Next Steps Exploration Worksheet — Other than your *Calling Star* itself, no worksheet deserves more attention and necessitates more self-honesty. These two tools are the heart and soul of your coaching experience during Week 6. Make the **Next Steps Exploration Worksheet** (p. 121) your friend.

Serving Coach — You will be assigned a serving coach to help you assimilate and leverage the information, as well as make observations and add insights to your *Calling Star*.

Homework — Your Acts 3 Discovery experience is an investment in your future. God will honor your commitment to the pursuit of self-assessment and the opportunities to serve in alignment with your calling. Homework is no small part of this experience. When asked to pray for others, pray. Also, know they are praying for you. When asked to complete worksheets, give yourself fully to it. God will not miss the moment to speak to you through these tools and clarify who you are through these assessments.

MAXIMIZING YOUR ACTS 3 DISCOVERY EXPERIENCE

Prayer — There is no one like the Master to explain His masterpiece. Invite Him to talk. Commit to listening.

Preparation — All group members should commit to prepare in advance by working through the Homework assigned for each week. **You will not get where you want to go without completing the assessments and assigned worksheets**. There simply are no shortcuts to this experience. You should complete your assignments reflectively and prayerfully. Mastery of this material and a solid grasp of the aggregate picture that your *Calling Star* paints will yield massive rewards for the rest of your life. Don't cheat the process, yourself, or the people and plans you were designed to serve.

Scripture — Expect the Word to be relevant to you. Take the time to read the scriptures in each lesson, both before and after the lesson. Open your heart to the personal insights afforded by the texts of the lesson.

Questions — Submit to the power of a question. The questions of this study are designed to probe deeply and point boldly to issues you are wise to consider. Authenticity is an absolute must. You must make this a genuine experience. Appropriate respect for the questions will take you where you might not otherwise go, but need to. Ample space is included in the margins of each page to give you a place to jot notes and thoughts.

Discussion—When discussion within the group is open, overcome the temptation to be silent. Saying what you think out loud becomes a kind of declaration that leaves an impression on your soul. And someone else may need to hear what you think. Share your insights from the assessments without hesitation. You are surrounded by people who want you to succeed—people who are fascinated to hear your story. Share the meaningful insights that you discover. When it's time for one-on-one sharing, be prayerful about who that person will be. If you're married, talk through what you've learned at home. While you're in the group setting, give God a chance to expand your friend circles. Look for a same-gender person whose talk seems to resonate with you. Expect God to use your partner to confirm what you think and clarify those things about which you are uncertain.

Attendance—These lessons are designed to be a sequential experience. Make a personal commitment to attend every session with your peers. Because this is a shared experience, your friends are depending on your consistency to attend. Missing multiple sessions will subvert the process. Of course, emergencies cannot be helped. If multiple sessions must be missed, please talk through the challenges with your facilitator. Upon request, there are alternate means to makeup missed sessions. If unavoidable interruptions are experienced, it is better to repeat the process than to shortchange it.

Arrival—We advise you to arrive 10 minutes before the scheduled start of a meeting. Feeling rushed will affect the experience. The informality of those few minutes before the meeting creates a rich environment in which to get comfortable with your peers and to develop new friendships. That extra 10 minutes will prove to be a cheap price for a valuable return.

DISCOVERY CONTENT ICONS

CALLING STAR highlights one of the primary personal traits that form the aggregate picture of the masterpiece God has designed you to be.

DISCUSSION highlights dialogue among the entire discovery group. It can be times of personal introduction or group interaction on designated issues. Except for introductions, personal sharing is encouraged, but not required.

TABLE TALK highlights dialogue among subsets of the Discovery Cohort. Sharing is highly encouraged at a cursory level.

PERSONAL SHARING highlights dialogue between 2-3 participants at a deeper level. Same gender pairing is preferred in order to encourage potential

accountability friendships.

 **SCRIPTURE** highlights Bible passages foundational to the teaching points and personal assessments.

 CONCEPT IMAGERY highlights object lessons used to teach Acts 3 Discovery principles.

 **PRAYER TIME** highlights opportunities to break into pairs or triplets for specific points of prayer and establish a framework for ongoing prayer.

 **HOMEWORK** highlights the steps that require your prayerful reflection and completion between meetings. Assessments, worksheets, and *Calling Star* development are crucial to the discovery process.

 GOING DEEPER highlights the material that we believe to be very helpful in the discovery process, but which can't be covered within the time constraints of our meeting times.

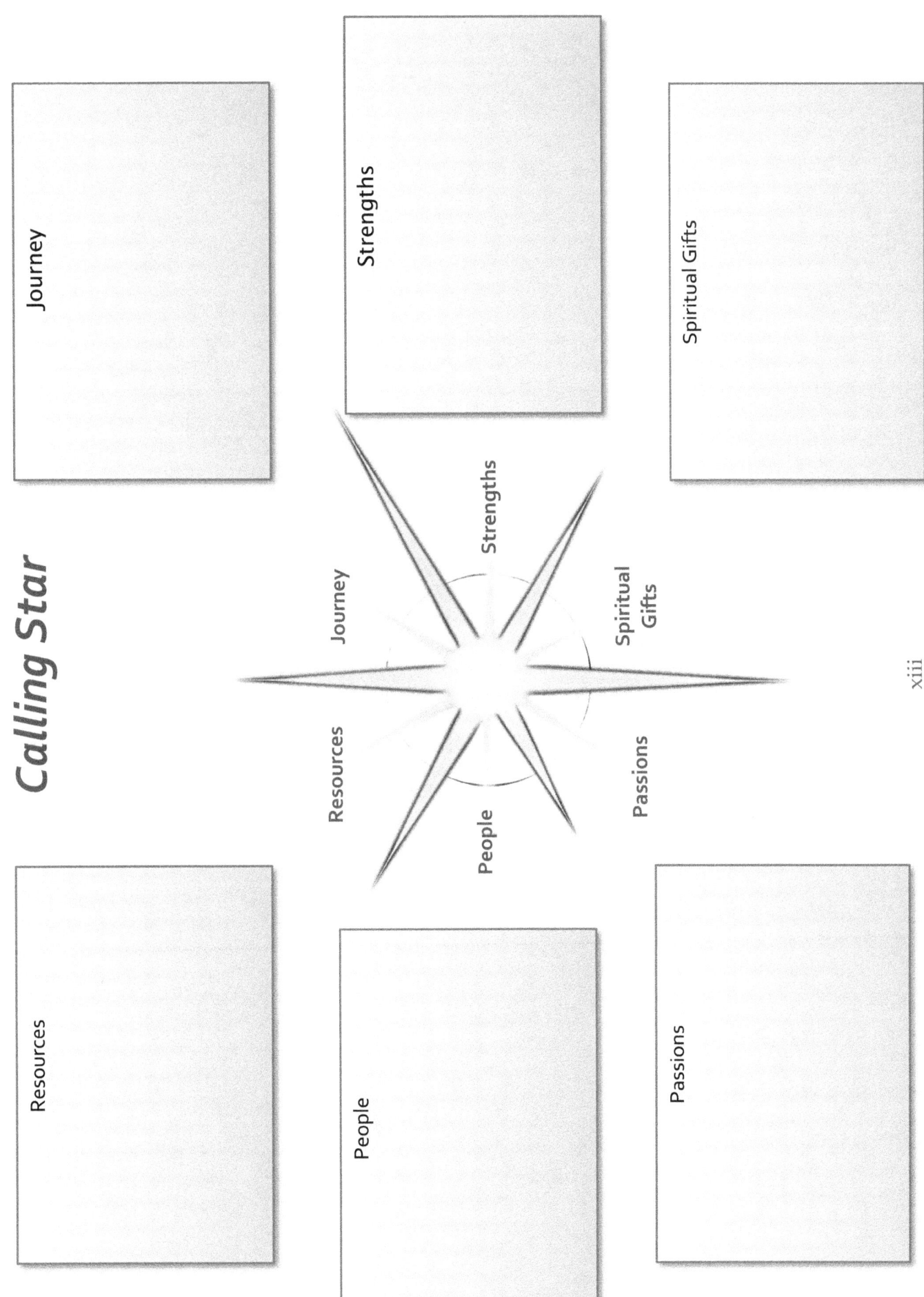

Week 1: Regaining Your Bearings

OPENING PRAYER

WELCOME TO ACTS 3 DISCOVERY

 ## PERSONAL INTRODUCTIONS (ROUND I)

Welcome to Week *One* of Acts 3 Discovery! We are so excited to embark on this exciting journey *together!* To get started, please share your name, a little bit about your family, and your work/career.

GUIDANCE FOR A NEW JOURNEY
You're not the first to look to Heaven for your next step

You are faced with countless choices and decisions every day. Some are easy—others are complex. Whether you find yourself in a new stage of life, or being intentional about making the most of your current stage, we are continuously making life-directing decisions. To help you through this transformational process, you need the right information, practical tools, and strong support to gain clarity and execute what God has in store for you. That's why ACT3 Ministry exists. We do not want you to be surprised or anxious about change. Instead, we want to serve as a mentor and advocate on your behalf. The heart of our mission is to give you a clarifying confidence of your divine calling and a pathway to connect that calling to meaningful opportunities to serve.

Acts 3 Discovery Participant Guide

THE FOUR STAGES OF LIFE AS CHARACTERIZED BY THEIR DISTINCTIVE FEATURES

1st Stage	**2nd Stage**	**3rd Stage**	**4th Stage**
Preparing Years	Building Years	Investing Years	Reflecting Years

Life Span

Stage 1: The Preparing Years
- Infancy to adolescence; birth – early 20's
- The season of play, imitation, and education
- Later stage transitions of enlarging world, growing independence, early life-directing decisions

Stage 2: The Building Years
- Emerging adulthood to adulthood; early 20's - early 50's
- The season of building careers, building family, building resumes, building assets
- High challenges of time management
- Commonly the most stressful stage
- Frequently the most challenging season to maintain psychological health in accepting a natural transition to the 3rd Stage

Stage 3: The Investing Years
- Midlife to older adulthood; early 50's to frail and elderly
- Family role transitions, career focus shifts from success to significance
- Legacy and generational impact

- A growing recognition of the potential impact of using your resources, capacities, and experiences to make a difference in the people and circumstances in the world around you, accompanied by a growing desire to make it happen

Stage 4: The Reflecting Years
- Frail and elderly
- High impact when modeling gratitude, encouraging family, friends, former associates, and mentees

Transition Concept:
- There are seasons of life between the definitive seasons in which life is lived with a foot in both worlds. As with any step naturally, the process starts with a lead step in which weight is transferred forward. With time, energy, and evolving purposes, the weight shifts to increase on the lead foot and decrease on the back foot until the next step is taken forward.

 **What would you add or modify to these characterizations of the seasons?**

Where do you see yourself on the 4 Stages of Life graphic?

What shifts do you see or sense are approaching for you personally?

What emotions do these considerations invoke in you?

THE FOUR STAGES OF LIFE AS A RELATIONSHIP BETWEEN DISCRETIONARY TIME AND AVAILABLE ENERGY

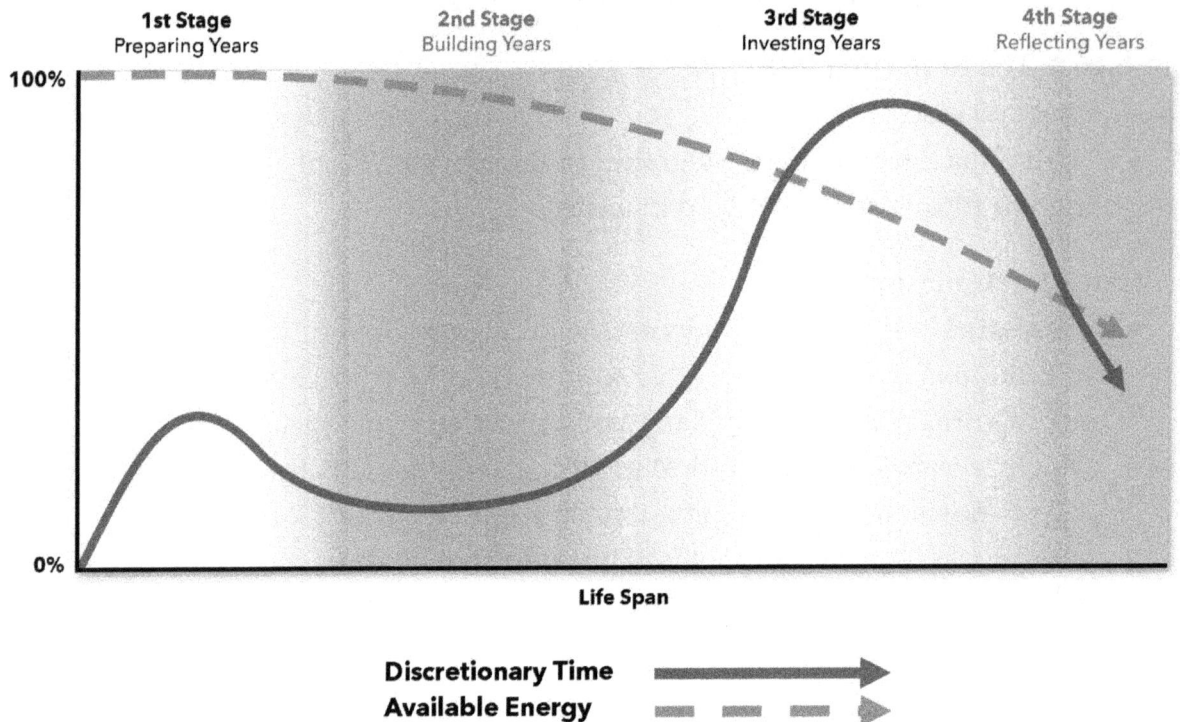

Definition of Discretionary Time: Designated activity is a matter of choice based on values and preferences, not predetermined commitments, such as vocation and family responsibilities.

Definition of Available Energy: The demands of life take their toll on the body physically, and God designed the human experience to, with time, normally decline cognitively, in stamina, and in recuperative capacities.

How would you modify the proposed trajectory of both Discretionary Time and Available Energy through the stages of life across an entire life time? Consider penciling in your own past, present, and projected considerations.

Where do you see yourself on these two factors at this point in your life?

INTRODUCTION TO YOUR CALLING STAR
Know where you are headed

The adventurous, daring, and brave have always relied on a guide. Before GPS, maps, and compasses, travelers found stars that could point the way—none worthier and more admired than the North Star.

> *"Calling is the spur that keeps us journeying purposefully – and thus growing and maturing – to the very end of our lives."*
>
> Os Guinness, English author and social critic

The disciples were at a loss as to how they would get to where Jesus was calling them to go after He was resurrected. He reassured them with the promise to give them His Guide—the Holy Spirit—to help them navigate their assigned course.

Among the beautiful stories of the Advent is that of the Wise Men and the most famous of all stars—"His Star" as they called it. There were probably countless stars out that night stretching over a moonlit sky, but one Guiding Star shone brightly over all the others to signify that the world had changed in a moment. This Star led these guys from their distant home to the front door of the King they sought to worship—a child still no older than a toddler and completely dependent on His parents, Joseph and Mary. They were looking for the proverbial needle in a haystack, but the Star gave them directions to their destination. And at His feet they offered their worship—the gifts Father God provided in advance to meet the needs of Jesus' family during a difficult time.

As the disciples and Wise Men required a guiding star to lead them to their calling, so do we! ACT3 Ministry uses a unique tool entitled *Calling Star* to help you identify the key considerations in your search to find next steps, best practices, and opportunities to serve in alignment with your calling. Your *Calling Star* is a composite picture of six distinct, yet related personal attributes that give insight to how God has wired you, where you have been, and where He wants to take you in order to fulfill His purpose for your life.

YOUR *CALLING STAR*

JOURNEY: The story of your significant life events and experiences

STRENGTHS: Your natural talents (abilities, behaviors, and ways of thinking) with which you were born

SPIRITUAL GIFTS: "Others-focused" talents given by the Holy Spirit upon accepting Christ

PASSIONS: The good things that make your heart sing and the bad things that break your heart

PEOPLE: Those who have spoken into your life and those who are speaking into your life now, and the notable things they said to you which impacted how you think and live your life yet today

RESOURCES: Time (the 168 hours available to you each week and how you use them) and Skills (the abilities you've honed to do something well)

Each week of study within your Acts 3 Discovery Cohort is designed to help you dive deeper into these six points of your *Calling Star* and explore them both individually and collectively. We believe the Holy Spirit will enlighten you as you reflect on each point in a way that perhaps you have never considered before.

JOURNEY: THE STORY OF YOUR SIGNIFICANT LIFE EVENTS AND EXPERIENCES.

What Paul wrote to the believers in Rome in Romans 8:28 was meant as more than reassurance that the frustrating circumstances in their lives would finally work out in the end. The key word is *everything*—God causes *everything* to work together for the good of those who love God and are called according to His purpose for them. You are no exception. The **Journey** point of your *Calling Star* comes into focus as you follow the outlined steps in the **Journey Map Worksheet** (p. 107) exercise that we will discuss soon. Here you will spend time reflecting on how God has used your experiences to shape your life, led you to where you are, and prepared you for every stage and its accompanying assignments for the rest of your life.

STRENGTHS: YOUR NATURAL TALENTS (ABILITIES, BEHAVIORS, AND WAYS OF THINKING) WITH WHICH YOU WERE BORN.

David, the Psalmist, declared that God had created his inmost being—that God had knit him together in his mother's womb. David praised God because, as his Creator, He had made him wonderfully complex and that His workmanship was marvelous. Again, you are no exception. God wove your personality and natural talents into your DNA long before you prayed to receive new life in Christ. Your strengths and talents determine how you will go about doing what He has purposed to do through you. The **Strengths** point of your *Calling Star* comes into focus through the personality assessment that will help you discover and understand your natural ways of thinking, identifying and solving problems, as well as relating to and working with other people.

SPIRITUAL GIFTS: "OTHERS-FOCUSED" TALENTS GIVEN BY THE HOLY SPIRIT UPON ACCEPTING CHRIST.

Natural strengths and talents are given before your first breath, but spiritual gifts are not given until after a person asks in faith for new life from Jesus Christ. Those gifts are given to a confessing believer because of what God has purposed to do through that person. Paul says that you are no exception—spiritual gifts are given to each of us so we can help each other. The **Spiritual Gifts** point of your *Calling Star* comes into focus through a spiritual gifts assessment that will allow you to discover or reaffirm the gifts the Holy Spirit has given to you.

PASSIONS: THE GOOD THINGS THAT MAKE YOUR HEART SING AND THE BAD THINGS THAT BREAK YOUR HEART.

Passions—fires in the belly—are built as we get exposed to the realities of our world. There are good things in our world for which we are driven to protect and promote. There are harmful things in our world, which we cannot tolerate or allow to go unchecked. The disciples recognized the presence and power of a personal passion in Jesus when He saw the abuses that were taking place in the Temple. They saw that it was eating Him alive. Jesus couldn't stand the thought that His Father's house was less than God intended. He couldn't live with those abuses He witnessed which dishonored His Father and hurt people. You are no exception in the capacity to "burn with a passion" deep inside of you. The **Passions** point of your *Calling Star* comes into focus as you work through a set of questions designed to challenge your thinking and to help you discover what makes, and what breaks, your heart.

PEOPLE: THOSE WHO HAVE SPOKEN INTO YOUR LIFE AND THOSE WHO ARE SPEAKING INTO YOUR LIFE NOW.

We need more than traveling companions. We need trusted people God can use to speak over and into our lives. Jesus convinced Saul of Tarsus that he was way off course in life. Jesus chose a person named Ananias to help him see his next steps at this critical point

Week 1: Regaining Your Bearings

in his journey. There is always a human component in God's system of giving His servants insight into their journey. You are no exception. The **People** point of your *Calling Star* comes into focus as you reflect on those people whom God has used in your life—past and present—and as we challenge you to open up to the possibility of adding to that list in the future.

RESOURCES: A SOURCE OF SUPPLY THAT CAN BE DRAWN UPON IN ORDER TO ACHIEVE A DESIRED OUTCOME.

Two resources that could particularly inform your place to serve are **Time** and **Skills**.

TIME: *The 168 hours available to you each week and how you use them.*

On day one of Creation, God created light and separated it from darkness. Though unstated, that one act also created time—the evening and the morning were the first day. After an unfathomable amount of creating on days two and three, God placed the sun, moon, and stars on the fourth day. The Bible clarifies that one of the purposes of those luminaries was to serve as signs to mark seasons and days and years. God meant for us to measure time and use it insightfully. Ecclesiastes teaches that there is a time for everything, and a season for every activity under Heaven. You are no exception. The **Time** contribution to your *Calling Star* comes into focus as you examine how you currently allocate your time and consider the possible redistribution of your time for the future.

SKILLS: *The ability to do something well; expertise.*

Skills are distinct from **Strengths** and **Spiritual Gifts**, yet they are still beautiful expressions of God's handiwork in your life. David was uniquely skilled as a musician, as well as a warrior. Exodus 31 tells of two men so gifted with craftsmanship that God personally chose them to build His Tabernacle for wilderness worship and the furniture that was made in the pattern of real objects in the Throne Room of Heaven. The **Skills** contribution to your *Calling Star* comes into focus as you identify the skills you have developed over time.

JOURNEY: THE STORY OF YOUR SIGNIFICANT LIFE EVENTS AND EXPERIENCES.

Take a road trip down memory lane from the past to understand the present

Everyone has a story. Everyone has had experiences in their life—some good and some not so good—which helped shape them into the person they are today. You are no exception. Understanding who you are and how you came to be that way is one of the keys to successfully identifying where you can serve best. Many of the behaviors, preferences, and priorities you personally express in your life today are rooted in your past experiences, along with your response to them.

This insightful exercise asks you to examine some of these life lessons by creating a visual representation—an actual map—of your life journey. Your **Journey Map** (p. 107) will prove to be foundational to your understanding of God's work in your life and His preparation for the purposes He has, and will continue, to assign you for your lifetime.

HOMEWORK

- Spend time answering the discussion questions at the conclusion of the teachings on the Four Stages of Life Graph and the Bell Curve Graph.

- Begin to build your **Journey Map** (p. 107).

- Exchange name tags and prayer requests and then pray for that person's Discovery experience and prayer request every day next week.

CLOSING PRAYER

Week 2: ReFocusing Your Heart

WELCOME TO ACTS 3 DISCOVERY

OPENING PRAYER

JOURNEY MAP PROGRESS

Please update us on your progress on this vital step. Ask for any clarification you need or for steps to get unstuck. Be encouraged to share your methods and or insights you've already gained.

THE HEART OF ACTS 3 DISCOVERY

Ephesians 1:15-19
For this reason, ever since I heard about your faith in the Lord Jesus and your love for all the saints, ¹⁶I have not stopped giving thanks for you, remembering you in my prayers. ¹⁷I keep asking that the God of our Lord Jesus Christ, the glorious Father, may give you the Spirit of wisdom and revelation, so that you may know Him better. ¹⁸I pray also that the eyes of your heart may be enlightened in order that you may know the hope to which He has called you, the riches of His glorious inheritance in the saints, ¹⁹and His incomparably great power for us who believe.

Our prayer for you is exactly like Paul's prayer for his Ephesian friends—people just like you—people with a lasting faith, a passionate love for others, and a deep understanding of God's grace. Why? We are praying these four principles for you:

1. To know _____

Two primary Greek words are translated into English as "know." The first is a fact-based knowledge that comes with observation and exposure to facts (I know your name). The second is the word that Paul uses in verse 17 because he wants to stress an intimate, experiential kind of knowledge (I am coming to know you). This "intimacy" requires more than just head knowledge; it requires a heart knowledge. It calls for an increasing awareness in hearing His voice more clearly and learning how to distinguish it, even when many others are speaking. Paul says this personal understanding of God and His presence will happen as God gives you the Spirit of wisdom and revelation.

FINDING YOUR "AHA!"
Discovering and discerning those God moments that breathe new life into your journey

As Paul continues to pray for his friends in Ephesus, he switches to another Greek word still best translated into English with the word "know." He chose the word for use in verse 18 and extends it to include the end of the sentence finished at the beginning of verse 19. This particular Greek word reveals those deeply desirable qualities noted are obtained in a slightly different manner and inferred to be qualities that grow with every observation or insight.

In this day of vastly improving technology, we've come to recognize differing capacities for the sharpness of the picture on a TV or a camera. The more pixels available with a device, the sharper the image. In effect, Paul is praying for exposures to God that enhance the knowledge "about God:" what He has in mind for them, how He feels about them, and how magnificent He is. Every experience brings greater clarity.

So, to this growing knowledge of God is added a powerful trilogy of life changing "AHA!" moments about God. Paul was certainly no stranger to unexpected, inspirational, and yes, sometimes-painful insights that completely dismantled what he knew and took him in a different direction. The dramatic conversion of Saul of Tarsus to Paul the Apostle was the first of many that would alter his course, allowing him to encounter countless "light bulb" moments. This lifetime of connecting-the-dots paved the way for Paul to walk through the door of hope and unlock many learning experiences to know God on a much more intimate level.

THE APERTURE OF THE HEART
Finding your Kodak Moment

Paul prays for the "eyes" to be enlightened for those who have experienced Jesus. In today's world, Paul might have used the term "aperture," describing the opening of light into a camera that is exposed to a film and burns an image into a picture on the soul. When a photographer wants to capture an image, he or she clicks the button that opens the shutter, allowing light through the aperture to leave an impression and create a photo—that "Kodak Moment."

Paul is praying that the aperture of your heart, the place the Bible describes as the seat of your emotions and the place decisions are made, would open up to the powerful light of Heaven and burn an eternal picture into your heart that you will never forget. Why? So that the picture of God's purpose may lead *you*, rather than all of the distractions that work to control your life, sap your energy, and subvert God's plans.

2. To know _____

It has been said that the most important day of your life is the day you were born and that the second most important day is when you discover why. The answer to that question changes everything! How do you find out and unleash the *why*? The journey to answering this profound, life-altering question leads you to *hope*, which is fuel for your calling.

A calling from God is like a "summons of the soul" where He directs your attention to a place He wants you to be or a mission He assigns you to undertake. God created you to be unique! That is why He speaks specifically to you. However, there will be challenges. You may have doubts and fears about your strengths and weaknesses. But do not be discouraged—rather, be encouraged! God is giving you new insights and revelations. God is calling you.

God is choosing you. God is commissioning you to step to a new cadence. Let's take a look at what the Scripture says:

- *...I have called him. I will bring him, and he will succeed in his mission. (Isa. 48:15)*

- *"For I know the plans I have for you," declares the Lord, "plans to prosper you and not to harm you, plans to give you hope and a future." (Jer. 29:11)*

- *I urge you to live a life worthy of the calling you have received. (Eph. 4:1)*

- *...For God's gifts and His call are irrevocable. (Rom. 11:29)*

3. To know _____

How do you know that you are valuable to God? For starters, it begins in the Manger at the joyful birth of a baby and continues with the revelation of God's love at the Cross. But it does not stop there. There are countless verses that demonstrate how God wonderfully sees you, such as:

- *You are God's workmanship — a masterpiece of His own hands. (Eph. 2:10)*

- *You are fearfully and wonderfully made. (Ps. 139:14)*

- *He chose you before the foundation of the world! (Eph. 1:11)*

- *We have different gifts, according to the grace given us. (Rom. 12:6)*

4. To know _____ available to live out your calling

This is best used to describe the most powerful event that has ever happened — the resurrection of Jesus Christ. Paul says this same mighty power that God exercised to raise Jesus from the dead is available to *you*. Yes, this life-changing power lives within you!

- You may feel that life is slipping you by and that your best "life-giving" days are over. But this incomparably great power exceeds the power of death in any of life's circumstances. Expect transformation and pursue spiritual growth. Your best days are ahead of you!

- You may feel that you have lost any position or platform to make a difference. But this incredibly great power not only raised Jesus from the dead, but "seated" Him in a position high enough to do exactly what the Father called Him to do. This same power can seat you—position you, exactly where God needs you to be, bringing clarity and purpose to your life!

- You may feel like all hell is breaking loose when the spirit of chaos and confusion challenges your every step. The enemy does not want you to fulfill your calling, much less hear the Voice of God. However, do not fear the enemy's deception, which causes confusion and doubt. This incomparably great power has already defeated Satan and every demon of Hell who collectively tried to stop Jesus. Rest assured, they couldn't stop Him—and that same power will keep them from stopping you!

To sum it all up, as you continue to grow in your relationship with God and find the "next steps" of your calling and purpose, it is crucial that you intimately recognize four valuable lessons. You need to:

1. KNOW God better than you do right now

2. KNOW God's calling for you

3. KNOW the value God places on you

4. KNOW the power He has made available to you

PRAYING TOGETHER

Ephesians 1:17-19 (paraphrased)
God, I ask you to bless _____. I pray that you would give _____ the Spirit of wisdom and revelation, so that (he/she) may know You better. I pray also that the eyes of _____ heart may be enlightened in order that (he/she) may know the hope of (his/her) calling, and that (he/she) may know the value You place on (him/her), and that

Acts 3 Discovery Participant Guide

_____ *may know Your incomparably great power at work in (him/her) as (he/she) believes. In Jesus name I pray. Amen!*

 HOMEWORK

- Pray Eph. 1:17-19 prayer (card provided) for each member of the Discovery Cohort individually at some point through the coming week. Pray for two different people each day.

- Spend time prayerfully reflecting on your life experiences and continue to develop your **Journey Map Worksheet** (p. 107). At any point you can begin to transfer those experiences into a visual **Journey Map**. This step will commemorate the life-shaping events and people God has used in your life in the shaping of who you are as His Masterpiece and the preparation for how He wants to use you in your life.

CLOSING PRAYER

Week 3: ReThinking Your Path

WELCOME AND OPENING PRAYER

FINDING YOUR WAY
It starts with how you think

We are living longer and healthier lives. According to experts, 3rd Stagers in the Investing years can expect to live another 20-30 years of reasonable healthiness following retirement, let alone the empty nest era, especially due to advances in technology and improvements in healthier lifestyles. At the same time, 3rd Stagers are increasingly unwilling to drift into personal irrelevance.

> *"We cannot solve our problems with the same thinking we used to create them."*
>
> — Albert Einstein

2nd Stagers in the Building years are not bereft of ways to stay busy. But they often do find themselves overwhelmed by options, driven by status, short of time, and running on fumes. Rarely does that need pointing out. But the chaos can cloud common sense and result in ruts that are the proverbial "graves without endwalls."

1st Stagers in the Preparing years find themselves with lengthening leashes and growing independence on one hand, and a growing uneasiness of stepping into the world of personal responsibility and accountability. How does fun and freedom get traded in for the next gear of life that requires producing out of the preparations? What are the next steps in life that provide for a strong start to the Building years?

How do you fight the strong currents of self-centeredness and the cultural mindset of leisurely pursuit that can sweep you exactly where you don't want to go? How do you get honest with yourself about your choices and use of your time, talents, and treasures and not wake up with that sand running out of the hour glass and booting you unprepared for the next season of life?

It all starts with how you think. It's pretty simple, really. If you want to be different, you have to think differently. Want to see a change? Change the way you think.

No person in history had to endure a more radical mindset change than Saul of Tarsus as he became the Apostle Paul. From being blinded by the Darkness to being blinded by the Light. From actively persecuting Christians to being persecuted and imprisoned himself. Changing from a zealot as a Roman citizen and Pharisee to being zealous for the souls of lost people. Converted from being an advocate of legalism to being a champion of grace. *Everything changed*. No wonder the Holy Spirit used Paul to challenge the Christians at Rome to think differently. He had experienced the ultimate of mindset transformations.

THE CALL TO RETHINK THE PATH FORWARD

Romans 12:2
Do not conform any longer to the pattern of this world, but be transformed by the renewing of your mind. Then you will be able to test and approve what God's will is – His good, pleasing, and perfect will.

There are no stronger commands from God than "Do not" and "Let there be." Therefore, when God says, "*Do not* be conformed" and "*be* transformed," you can rest assured that change is in the works.

The contemporary term for "pattern of this world" is _____.

> Paul is most likely not thinking about big sin issues here, but rather those that are common sense, simple matters of obedience. He has their core values and priority lists in mind—how they view their material possessions, their personal freedoms, and the needs of others.

Week 3: ReThinking Your Path

Conformation is taking the shape of _____ and putting the squeeze on who you are at the very heart of what matters inside.

Conformation starts with external pressures, but eventually shapes what we think and do. In today's world, we hear the constant drumbeat of do your own thing…it's okay because everyone else—from the famous to your friends—is doing it. We constantly struggle with rationalizing our thoughts and actions. The effect is usually temporary, yet constantly taking on new shapes, because as soon as the pressure points change, like all trends or fashions do, how we think and what we do changes, too.

Transformation is an inside job that converts your _____ and _____.

Transformation starts by changing how we think. Forgiveness and salvation start with a change of thinking on our part and are demonstrated in our confession and repentance. Transformation must start with confession of our wrong thinking and conformity in subtle ways to the "norms" of our world. Transformation must include repentance and a commitment to a new approach to living.

WHAT WE MIGHT RETHINK

- What are the cultural norms for your stage? How do these differ inside the church?

- How might the Holy Spirit want us to ReTHINK these norms?

THE NEED TO RETHINK THE PATH YOU'VE WALKED

1 Peter 1:1-2
Peter, an apostle of Jesus Christ, to God's elect, strangers in the world, scattered throughout Pontus, Galatia, Cappadocia, Asia, and Bithynia, ²who have been chosen according to the foreknowledge of God the Father, through the sanctifying work of the Spirit, for obedience to Jesus Christ and sprinkling by His blood.

Shifting family dynamics; considering, entering, or enjoying a form of retirement; an evolving social world — these are all markers of life flux. If only one word were used to describe those markers of life, it would have to be *transition*. Life often brings unwelcomed monumental change and a tsunami of feelings and emotions. Transition exposes us to the soul-jarring questions of "Who am I now? How did I get here? Why am I here?" Are you prepared for the answers?

In the Scripture above, Peter comes alongside a group of disoriented believers to help them regain their bearings. They had not braced themselves for the realities of their displacement from the familiar, and they were a little dazed by their "new normal." With the first strokes of the pen in his first letter, Peter stabilizes his friends' thinking by challenging them to rethink their answers to the same haunting questions we find ourselves asking: How did I get here and where is God in this?

Even though you may have doubts, God has _____.

To be chosen by God involves thoughtful and deliberate consideration by Him, in the spirit of His kindness, favor, mercy, and love. God not only has a plan for the world, He has a plan just for *you*. He has a mission with your name on it to help carry out His plan. You just need to answer the call.

The transitions of life can make you feel _____.

The people and culture that Peter addresses are the exact same ones that give rise to Fiddler on the Roof and its iconic song: *Tradition!* Papa, mama, sons, and daughters know their verses, as well as the tune. What's more, after centuries of exile, Jews find ways to get back to their promised land. No small part of their identity is their homeland.

When Peter calls these God-chosen people *strangers*, he hits a raw nerve and undoubtedly causes personal pain. It is a powerful word for Peter to use to describe these believers. It emphasizes a transitional state. Peter's choice of the word acknowledges that their feet are not standing where their roots are firmly planted and their current home is not where their heart is.

The original Greek word describes a resident-foreigner. For some in today's world, traveling or moving to a different country is an exciting adventure. For others, it can feel unfamiliar, awkward, and even stressful just walking down the street or getting in a taxi. This word describes someone, not simply traveling, but living in a foreign culture—like that proverbial "fish out of water" feeling when faced with new smells, sounds, textures, faces, places, and mores.

You have not been randomly tossed into life, but rather God has _____.

Don't miss Peter's choice to use the word *scattered*. At first glance to us, this well-known farming term in biblical days may sound like a discombobulated flinging of seed. Oh my, you would be overlooking one of the powerful messages Peter wanted these struggling believers to get!

Remember that Peter was addressing people living in an agrarian culture. With wide-eyed wonder, they would have read that word we have translated into English as *scattered*. In actuality, it is a perfect choice of words, if you want to convey a sense of intentionality and strategy.

PRECISION PLANTING
Understanding God's Strategic Placement of His People

As a present-day illustration of God's people-farming prowess, a Midwest grain farmer plants a quarter of a billion corn and bean seeds every spring. When using the latest technology described as prescription farming, the farmer knows everything required to make an informed decision as to the planting of each seed. He knows the genetics of the seed, exactly where the seed is being planted in the field, the soil type in that part of the field, the optimum spacing between each seed in that particular soil, and the exact depth the seed should be planted for the weather conditions. Why? For maximum production in his fields come harvest time.

God's plan is to use you where you are, however you think you got there.

God is looking at the end of our life from the very beginning, our personal planting, if you will. He knows where He wants you, how to get you there, and how to use you right where you are today!

These believers are many miles from their ancestral homeland. They obviously felt uncomfortable where they were living. They likely were worried about the impact it would have on their children and on future generations. With this familiar term, Peter changes their perspective and raises their hopes. He tells them they have been intentionally planted exactly where God had intended them to be all the time! They can be blessed and have eternal impact, where they are.

THE MODEL FOR RETHINKING

Philippians 2:5-8
Let this mind be in you which was also in Christ Jesus, ⁶who, being in the form of God, did not consider it robbery to be equal with God, ⁷but made Himself of no reputation, taking the form of a bondservant, and coming in the likeness of men. ⁸And being found in appearance as a man, He humbled Himself and became obedient to the point of death, even the death of the cross. (NKJV)

The perfect model for ReThinking is Jesus. No one has ever more perfectly followed through with the plans of Father God. No one has ever had to adjust more to the reality of changing circumstances in order to complete His assignment. And no one has ever had such impact on the world because of the adjustments so willingly made.

The watershed mindset of Jesus, and His humble obedience deserves a deeper dive on your part. We will help you go there by spending time in the Going Deeper section at the end of this session.

This challenge is no easy feat. But Paul understood the need for a reset of our thinking. And Paul wanted his dear friends to experience the fullest potential of their lives. This passage is not just the setting of a standard; it can become the powerful cry of your heart, both for yourself, as well as the people in your life.

PRAYING TOGETHER

Phil 2:5-8 (paraphrased)
Father God, I pray that You will help _____ to have the same mind – the same kind of thinking – which was also in Christ Jesus, who, being in the form of God, did not consider it robbery to be equal with God. Like you did, Jesus, help _____ to make himself/herself of no reputation. Help him/her to take on the form of a bondservant. Now, as a bondservant, I pray that you will help him/her to be humble and live obediently to YOUR revealed will to his/her last breath. In Jesus name, Amen!

HOMEWORK

- Finalize your **Journey Map** (p. 107) and bring it with you next week.

- During your quiet time this week, use the Going Deeper Guide at the end of this session to reflect on Philippians 2:5-8 and ask the Holy Spirit to help you think about Jesus as a model for ReTHINKING.

- Use the provided card to pray the Philippians 2:5-8 prayer for each member of the Discovery Cohort individually at some point through the coming week. Pray for two different people each day.

CLOSING PRAYER

GOING DEEPER

 *Philippians 2:5-8*
Let this mind be in you which was also in Christ Jesus, ⁶who, being in the form of God, did not consider it robbery to be equal with God, ⁷but made Himself of no reputation, taking the form of a bondservant, and coming in the likeness of men. ⁸And being found in appearance as a man, He humbled Himself and became obedient to the point of death, even the death of the cross. (NKJV)

The pathway to making life count is paved with sacrifice. We need a champion to show us the pathway to servanthood. Paul tells us to look no farther than Jesus. He is the model of ReThinking! Philippians 2:5-8 sums up the response of Jesus to His Father when asked to assume the most demanding assignment ever delegated.

From this passage (and other scriptures), how was the life of Jesus different for Him as a man on Earth, as compared to His life as the Son of God in Heaven?

- What were His prerogatives?
    - In Heaven?
    - On Earth?

- What were His limitations?
    - In Heaven?
    - On Earth?

- What was His status among those around Him?
    - In Heaven?
    - On Earth?

Note the differences. Paul wanted us to know that Jesus made a strategic decision to put Himself in the vulnerable position of Manhood. Circle the words in this passage that were personal choices on His part in order to fulfill His calling.

Reflect on the status and rights you've earned in your current stage of life and the benefits you have understandably anticipated as a result. If we ReTHINK our prerogatives, what strategic decisions might you have to make in order to live out God's purpose for you?

Week 4: Exploring the Impact of Your Journey

WELCOME AND OPENING PRAYER

PERSONAL SHARING
Sharing your Journey Map

If you are married and are blessed to have your spouse with you in this Cohort, we urge you to share your insights before or after the Cohort. During these interactions, please connect with a same gender person. It's a fun time to share your story and maybe make a new God-friend.

Please share an overview of your **Journey Map** (p. 107) with another Cohort friend over the next 25-30 minutes. Reflect on the following questions as you share your **Journey Map:**

- What did you learn, or confirm, about yourself by looking at your **Journey** in this way?

- What are three of the most impactful events of your life?

- How do those life-shaping events impact the way you live today? How might they impact your choices for the future?

- How can you see your **Journey** fitting into God's plan for you and His larger mission for the world?

 **HOMEWORK**

- Spend some time prayerfully reflecting on your **Journey Map** (p. 107). Ask the Holy Spirit to identify the most significant 3-5 life events, experiences, or "aha" moments that He has used to get you to where you are, as well as shape who you are and how you think. Write these experiences in the **Journey** point of your *Calling Star*.

- You will be sent a personal code to enable you to take a Gallup Strengths Assessment. The email providing your personal code will also contain instructions on how to access and complete the assessment. A 2nd email will follow providing instructions on how to access your reports. The purchase of the code makes all support material yours to download at any time after completion. If you need further instructions, please contact your facilitator.

- If you are married, share your **Journey Map** with your spouse. If they are not attending, it could be a wonderful testimony to them. If you have kids, your **Journey Map** could be a wonderful Faith Talk at some point, whatever their ages.

CLOSING PRAYER

Week 5: Admiring the Master's 1st Stroke

WELCOME AND OPENING PRAYER

STRENGTHS
Your natural talents (abilities, behaviors, and ways of thinking) with which you were born

Ephesians 2:10
For we are God's workmanship, created in Christ Jesus to do good works, which God prepared in advance for us to do.

THE MASTER'S MARKINGS AND OUR PROVENANCE

At heart, artists want credit for their work. Painters leave their inscription. Potters leave their stamp. We should not be surprised to learn that the Great Artist leaves His Seal.

Like a master painter with all the colors of the palate and the tools of the trade at the artist's disposal, God has limitless options available to make us each uniquely beautiful and useful. The choices are His. Each stroke of the brush, every turn of the wheel, and every cut of the chisel is His to make. Out of all you could be, He created you intentionally to be who you are in Christ. He had purposes in mind when He did.

As the prayer of Ephesians 1 is the heart of the Acts 3 Discovery process, **Ephesians 2:10 is its foundation.** The twin pillars of **personal worth** and **individual purpose** rest firmly on the declaration that we are each the Master's masterpiece and that He created us with our purpose in mind.

Paul then declares in Ephesians 3 that redeemed and purpose-fulfilling people are an indisputable and eternal demonstration of His glory.

And the Great Artist's first act in creating you was early.

THE FIRST BRUSHSTROKE OF THE MASTER

Psalms 139:13-14
For You created my inmost being; You knit me together in my mother's womb. ¹⁴ I praise You because I am fearfully and wonderfully made.

David, the Psalmist, declared that God had created his inmost being—that *God had knit him together in his mother's womb. David praised God because, as his Creator, He had made him wonderfully complex and that His workmanship was marvelous.* You are no exception. God wove your personality traits and natural talents into your DNA, long before you prayed to receive new life in Christ.

THE GENIUS OF THE MASTER CREATOR

Our personality and natural talents drive how we interact with people and solve problems.

The fascination with the human personality and natural talents is well documented for millennia. The multiple assessment tools that work to classify those traits all follow the study of the genius of our Master Creator.

The Master did not simply care about making us unique as an expression of His limitless creativity; He brilliantly created a social system that demanded mutual respect, relationship, and interdependence.

God designed us to want, enjoy, and need each other to maximize our human experience.

Since we are intentionally designed to be interdependent, we must find ways to get along with all kinds of people in all kinds of situations.

The Fall in the Garden created lots of problems, but among them is that we are naturally self-centered and want to be independent. God has specifically endowed and gifted some people with relational skills to connect and motivate others to counterbalance that general influence.

God knew we would have to solve the problems we encounter as we live out our lives in a broken world and work to find ways to make life better.

He knew the problems of a broken world would be complex and require more than any one person could bring to the table. So, He naturally endowed and cognitively gifted some people with the capacities to gather and process information with the intent to make decisions and design plans. To ensure that the plans are put into place, He also similarly capacitated some to energize themselves and others toward the execution of those plans and the desired results.

INTRODUCTION TO TALENTS & STRENGTHS

All people have a unique combination of talents, knowledge, and skills that they use in their daily lives to do their work, achieve their goals, and interact with others. While skills and knowledge can be acquired, you are born with your **Talents**. These naturally occurring behaviors, ways of thinking, personality nuances, and feelings are how you were fearfully and wonderfully made by God. When you spend time, energy, and other resources to grow your **Talents**, that is when those **Talents** become **Strengths**.

Can you think of someone who has a very clear God-given Talent who has invested in it to make it a Strength?

Even though we are all born with **Talents**, many people don't really know what their **Talents** are and therefore don't focus on using them every day. Instead, many people tend to focus on fixing their weaknesses or becoming someone that they are not created to be. By exploring your **Talents**, you can

> *Identifying your **Talents** is not intended to take the place of identifying your **Spiritual Gifts**, but rather, it can be a powerful way to enhance your gifts and calling.*
>
> Winesman, Clifton, and Leisveld

identify and build on the areas where you have infinite potential to grow and succeed as you look to fulfill your calling.

Those qualities, which your Heavenly Father infused into your unique temperament, have been detected and confirmed with your results from the personal strengths assessment. The **Strengths** point of your *Calling Star* comes into focus as you discover and understand your natural strengths and talents.

We are ready for a type of artistic critique of the work of the Master and His foundational strokes on the canvas of your life.

 **HOMEWORK**

- Prayerfully study the results of your strengths assessment (provided separately) and bring them with you next week.

CLOSING PRAYER

Week 6: Celebrating Your Strengths

WELCOME AND OPENING PRAYER

STRENGTHS
Your natural talents (abilities, behaviors, and ways of thinking) with which you were born

Please follow the instructions of your facilitator as they direct your grouping for sharing your strengths assessment. It is an affirming time to share your results, as well as a wonderful opportunity to learn more about your peers.

SHARING THE FINDINGS OF YOUR STRENGTHS ASSESSMENT

Please use the following questions as a guide to share your findings:

- Looking at the results of the strengths assessment you took, with which of your **Talents** do you most strongly identify? Why?

- Can you identify a time in life when you saw this **Talent** as a **Strength** that God leveraged?

- Just because these are our talents, it doesn't mean that we are always comfortable with our natural inclinations.
    - *Which of your talents is your favorite? Why?*

    - *Which of your talents can drive you (and perhaps sometimes others around you) crazy? Why?*

    - *Which talent have you heard about that you may wish you had more of? Why?*

PERSONAL STRENGTHS ASSESSMENT GROUP COACHING SEGMENT NOTES:

Acts 3 Discovery Participant Guide

DREAMING: OUT-OF-THE-BOX RETHINKING
Unlocking the heart

 *Acts 2:17*
In the last days, God says, "I will pour out my Spirit on all people. Your sons and daughters will prophesy, your young men will see visions, your old men will dream dreams."

The context of this verse was the exciting time of Pentecost in Jerusalem after Jesus had ascended back to Heaven. It is a powerful illustration of what can happen as our Ephesians 1:15-17 prayer gets answered! It was the day the *Spirit of wisdom and revelation* was "poured out," the Church was birthed, and believers were transformed and sent forth to bless the world.

The foundational prayer of your Acts 3 Discovery experience is Paul's prayer for the Ephesians. As the Spirit of wisdom and revelation helps you to know God better, your sensitivity to His plans for your life gets more detailed and your trust grows deeper for when He calls you beyond your comfort levels. Acts 2:17 sheds the light of expectation that God may have an **"out-of-the-box dream"** you've never dared to live before now. A dream doesn't have to be the latest, greatest ministry, but an insight that is new to you in how to respond to a need that has caught your heart. It could also be a dream you've never dared to share before now, and your heart is being freshly stirred to act.

 **TABLE TALK**

Have you ever had a sense that God has given you a dream—a task, or a sense of calling for a lifetime? What did it feel or look like? What gave you the sense that it included God's presence?

 **PRAYING TOGETHER**

Exchange nametags with someone at your table and pray for them.

- Ask what *one* thing you could pray for them this week that

Week 6: Celebrating Your Strengths

would be helpful.

- Pray that the Holy Spirit would renew them and help them to know their calling.

- Pray that they would discover opportunities to serve consistent with their calling.

 **HOMEWORK**

- Use the information you gathered from the person with whom you exchanged a nametag and pray for that person every day this week.

- Spend some time prayerfully reflecting on the personal strengths assessment you completed and complete the **Strengths Worksheet** (p. 109). Record the Top 5 Strengths in the **Strengths** point of your *Calling Star*.

- As you complete the **Strengths Worksheet**, go back to your **Journey Map** (p. 107). Ask the Holy Spirit to identify the times that He has used your **Strengths** to make a difference in His Kingdom.

- Complete the **Spiritual Gifts Assessment**. A link to an electronic version will be emailed to you this week. A hard copy is available upon request.

- Invest time in the Going Deeper session below.

CLOSING PRAYER

 ## GOING DEEPER

Balconies & Basements

Since talents come naturally to us, we must be aware that we can both under- and over-utilize **Talents** and even **Strengths**.

Go to YouTube and search for "Gallup Theme Thursday Short - Balconies and Basements Explained."

Week 7: Embracing Your Spiritual Gifts

WELCOME AND OPENING PRAYER

Spiritual Gifts are given by the Holy Spirit to serve the Church and advance the mission it has been assigned. The gifts reside in the individual, but belong to the Church for her benefit.

Recognition of the Spiritual Gifts the Holy Spirit has endowed and the guidance He promises will inevitably lead to both nurture and outreach. We are not waiting for the Spirit for spiritual gifts. He is waiting for us to use them!

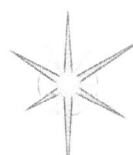

SPIRITUAL GIFTS
'Others-focused' talents given by the Holy Spirit upon accepting Christ

1 Corinthians 12:4-11
There are different kinds of gifts, but the same Spirit. ⁵There are different kinds of service, but the same Lord. ⁶There are different kinds of working, but the same God works all of them in all men. ⁷Now to each one the manifestation of the Spirit is given for the common good. ⁸To one there is given through the Spirit the message of wisdom, to another the message of knowledge by means of the same Spirit, ⁹to another faith by the same Spirit, to another gifts of healing by that one Spirit, ¹⁰to another miraculous powers, to another prophecy,

to another distinguishing between spirits, to another speaking in different kinds of tongues, and to still another the interpretation of tongues. ¹¹All these are the work of one and the same Spirit, and He gives them to each one, just as He determines.

We are introduced to God in the first verse of the Bible as the Creator of Heaven and Earth. That was not a one-and-done proposition for our Creator God. John records in John 5:17 that Jesus taught, *My Father is always at His work to this very day, and I, too, am working.*

Creator God caused the beauty of the universe and the awesome balance of nature. David wrote in Psalms 19:1, *The heavens declare the glory of God; the skies proclaim the work of His hands.* Careful study would confirm that His work in the heavens and on Earth is ongoing. That work is so structured and systematic that our study of His work is the foundation of all science.

Creator God is at work building the Church through Jesus Christ. Jesus told His disciples *on this rock I will build my Church...* The Church is the collection of God's people on Earth and the means through which He carries out His plans in the world. Though Pentecost was the birth of His Church, He continues to build it to this day. The ongoing work of Jesus includes building believers and fitting them into this beautiful and powerful body of people.

> *"When you find your spiritual gift, God will give you an opportunity to use it."*
>
> John Maxwell

And Creator God is at work shaping and fitting you into the Church. His work in you is about connecting you relationally with other believers and functionally in how you contribute in the work of the whole.

God's work on who we are and how we relate to others is His ongoing dedication to our maturity. His work to fit us into His purposes was planned before our first breath, and it

> *"God has given a spiritual gift to the church in you, and you dare not keep it to yourself."*
>
> Aaron Niequist

Week 7: Embracing Your Spiritual Gifts

was energized when we accepted Christ and we were filled with His Spirit.

Finding your fit is based on your understanding of how God has equipped you to best serve. So, finding your fit should therefore include a study of the **Spiritual Gifts**.

Michelangelo took years to sculpt David and paint the Sistine Chapel. God takes our lifetime to finish His work on us. But there are two major movements in God's work on you:

- The day you were given life and He fashioned your DNA from your parents. That day He determined the natural talents and abilities with which you would live your life.

- The day you were given eternal life through Faith and the gift of the Spirit. That day you were infused with Spiritual DNA, transmitting traits of your Heavenly Father which make you like Him through spiritual gifts.

If the concept of being given Eternal Life is new to you, or you would like to know more about how that can happen for you, we urge you to spend time Going Deeper with the reflective study at the end of this week's session.

In 1 Corinthians 12:4-11, Paul is describing what happens in the 2nd big movement of the Master in your life. As your DNA and personality traits form the basis for your resemblance to your earthly parents, your spiritual gifts form part of the basis of your resemblance to your Heavenly Father.

USING YOUR SPIRITUAL GIFTS

1 Peter 4:10
Each one should use whatever gift he has received to serve others, faithfully administering God's grace in its various forms.

Finding your assignments in this stage of your life must include reassurance of how He has wired you for service. Once you know your gifts,

> *"You are the only person on Earth who can use your ability."*
>
> Zig Ziglar

Peter is clear—you should use them! The purpose of the gifts is to serve others. When you serve, it is God working in real time in you. Letting God harness your natural strengths and employ your spiritual gifts to serve is the partnership God longs to experience with you.

Holy Spirit + Spirit-filled Church + your spiritual gift = meeting needs and completing mission

Serving with your spiritual gifts creates the profound opportunity for you to experience the unique partnership with the Holy Spirit ministering to a specific need. You become part of an equation that is unbalanced without your involvement. You can't take you out of the equation without impacting the outcome.

Personal maturity and repeated use do beautiful things to your **Spiritual Gifts**. When we use our gifts they blossom. Many are latent until they are activated by opportunities to serve which require them.

In a similar way, we may take an assessment at different times in our lives and the assessment reveals we have new gifts at work in our life. It may appear that God is giving us different gifts, when actually the gift has become more detectable because of use.

 **TABLE TALK: SHARING YOUR SPIRITUAL GIFTS**

- What are your **Spiritual Gifts**? Is this a new discovery or reaffirmation for you?

- What is one area where God has called you (either in the past or now) to use one of your **Spiritual Gifts**?

Week 7: Embracing Your Spiritual Gifts

 **HOMEWORK**

- Reflect on the results of your **Spiritual Gifts Assessment**. Record your top three **Spiritual Gifts** in your *Calling Star*.

- Review the Understanding Spiritual Gifts beginning on page 61.

- Review Spiritual Gifts Application Guide beginning on page 65.

- Spend time reviewing the Going Deeper study.

CLOSING PRAYER

 **GOING DEEPER**

ACCEPTING JESUS AND RECEIVING ETERNAL LIFE IN AND THROUGH HIM

"To reach our highest potential, to have abundant life, to receive forgiveness and be free from condemnation, to live in communion with Father God, and to find renewed purpose for living, we must accept Jesus Christ by faith." -Jack Hayford

The Roman's Road to Salvation outlines the essential steps toward understanding the Gospel message and receiving salvation through Jesus Christ. It clearly articulates the reality of sin, its consequences, the provision of salvation, and the response needed to accept God's free gift of eternal life. Pause for a moment and ask the Holy Spirit to help you understand these steps and lead you in how to embrace the truths they reveal and receive Jesus Christ as your Savior.

1. **The Universality of Sin**

   Romans 3:10 – "As it is written, 'There is none righteous, not even one.'"

   - This verse emphasizes that no one is inherently righteous. Every person is guilty of sin, and no one can make it right before God by their own efforts.

   Romans 3:23 – "For all have sinned and fall short of the glory of God."

   - We've disappointed ourselves, so it's no wonder we have sinned in the eyes of the Holy God. Every person has sinned and fallen short of God's perfect standard. Sin is universal and affects every human being, regardless of status or background.

2. **The Consequences of Sin**

   Romans 6:23 – "For the wages of sin is death, but the free gift of God is eternal life in Christ Jesus our Lord."

   - Sin carries a price: spiritual death and eternal separation from God. However, God offers eternal life as a free gift through faith in Jesus Christ.

3. **God's Love and Provision for Sinners**

   Romans 5:8 – "But God demonstrates His own love toward us, in that while we were yet sinners, Christ died for us."

   - Even though we are sinners, God loves us. His love was demonstrated by giving us His Son and through Jesus' sacrificial death on the cross. Jesus died in our place, bearing the punishment that we deserved, to reconcile us to God.

4. **Salvation Through Faith in Jesus**

   Romans 10:9-10 – "That if you confess with your mouth Jesus as Lord, and believe in your heart that God raised Him from the dead, you will be saved; for with the heart a person believes, and with the mouth he confesses, resulting in salvation."

   - Salvation is not earned by good works or religious deeds, but by believing in the death and resurrection of

Jesus Christ and confessing Him as Lord. This faith results in right standing with God and salvation that provides us eternal life.

Romans 10:13 – "For whoever will call on the name of the Lord will be saved."

- Salvation is available to anyone who sincerely calls upon the Lord in faith. It is not exclusive to a specific group or person but open to all who turn to Jesus in trust and an expressed sorrow for sin, which we call repentance.

5. **The Assurance of Peace with God**

Romans 5:1 – "Therefore, having been justified by faith, we have peace with God through our Lord Jesus Christ."

- Once we place our faith in Jesus, we are justified—declared righteous before God—and we have peace with Him. This peace is a reconciliation that assures us of our relationship with God through Jesus.

6. **No Condemnation for Those in Christ**

Romans 8:1 – "Therefore there is now no condemnation for those who are in Christ Jesus."

- For those who accept Jesus Christ as their Savior, there is no longer condemnation or judgment. Their sins are forgiven, and they are free from the penalty of sin.

The Roman's Road leads a person from the recognition of their sin and its consequences to the understanding that God, in His love, has provided a solution through Jesus Christ. By confessing we have sinned, declaring Jesus died for those sins, believing in His resurrection, and accepting Him as the Lord of our life, we receive the free gift of eternal life and assurance of our salvation. This journey points to God's grace, available to anyone who calls upon His name. By following the Roman's Road, believers and seekers alike are shown the simplicity and depth of the Gospel message. Through this, many have come to know the saving power of Jesus Christ.

If you have more questions, please talk to your facilitator or a spiritual leader in whom you have confidence. If you are ready to accept the teaching of Romans and express your need of and faith in

Jesus Christ, make the following prayer yours, or use your own words as you express your heart to God.

Prayer:

Father God, I know that I am a sinner and that I need you to forgive me. I believe that your son Jesus died a on the Cross and rose again so that my sins could be forgiven. Thank you. I want to make you the Lord of my life, and I will trust and follow You. I give myself to you right now. In the name of Jesus, amen.

Next Steps:

- If you prayed that prayer, your church and ACT3 Ministry celebrates that with you! Let us know.

- Please tell your facilitator and/or a friend in your Cohort as quickly as possible.

- If your Acts 3 Discovery Cohort is a part of the programing of a local church, please share your new faith in Jesus and relationship with God with a pastor or spiritual leader at the church. They will be your best friends in how to take the next steps in your new faith.

Week 7: Embracing Your Spiritual Gifts

Understanding Spiritual Gifts

Jesus was empowered by the Holy Spirit to do ministry as He lived out His purpose and served people while He was on Earth. Jesus made a mind-boggling statement that one day Christians would do even greater ministry than He did (John 14:2). Certainly, He never meant to infer that Christians are greater than Him. But He did lay the foundation for the future impact of the Church as each member would be individually gifted and empowered by the Holy Spirit, which would generate an exponential effect.

The Church is a team made up of people who are each uniquely equipped to minister like Jesus. Our personal ministry is therefore the continuation of Jesus' ministry. And the same Holy Spirit who empowered Him has endued you with some of the same abilities and power to serve today.

THE GIFTS

Spiritual gifts are discussed and listed in the following passages of the New Testament: 1 Corinthians 12:8-10; 12:28; Romans 12:6-8; Ephesians 4:11; and 1 Peter 4:11. **Since these lists are not duplicative, there are likely more gifts than the ones described in these passages.** *Additionally, for our purposes, ACT3 Ministry exists to connect people with opportunities to serve, which has resulted in our refined list that match most church teams and community service organizations.*

CATEGORIES OF SPIRITUAL GIFTS

The Apostle speaks of the variety of spiritual gifts: "Now there are different kinds of gifts, but the same Spirit. And there are different kinds of service, but the same Lord. There are different kinds of working, but the same God works all of them in all men... All of these are the work of one and the same Spirit, and He gives them to each one, just as He determines" (1 Corinthians 12:4-11).

In a study of spiritual gifts, it is helpful to recognize different categories of spiritual gifts that are described in Scripture:

- **Motivational Gifts**: How God works in a believer to shape his or her perspective on life and motivate his or her words and actions.

- **Ministry Gifts**: How God works with what a believer does to serve and meet the needs of others.

- **Manifestation Gifts**: How God works through a believer in a given situation to demonstrate His supernatural power.

Motivational Gifts

The motivational gifts include gifts such as: faith, prophecy, serving, teaching, exhorting, giving, organizing, and mercy. These gifts of God's grace shape how the believer views life, relates to others, and impacts the Body of Christ. A motivational gift can be compared to a set of eyeglasses from God, given so that the believer can see people and circumstances through that particular set of "lenses."

Following are simple descriptions of motivational gifts, explaining how a person with each gift would "see" his or her role in the Body of Christ:

- Faith: Takes the lead and encourages others in acting on God's promises with confidence and unwavering belief in God's ability to fulfill His purposes.

- Prophecy: Reveals truth by exposing sin, so that fellowship with God can be restored and/or maintained.

- Serving/Helping: Demonstrates love by meeting practical needs, usually through tangible work.

- Teaching: Discovers and validates truth so that the Church maintains accuracy.

- Encouragement: Encourages Christians to grow spiritually by discipling, teaching, and counseling others.

- Giving: Conserves and shares resources in order to meet needs.

- Leadership: Carries out projects by recruiting workers, organizing tasks, or delegating responsibilities.

- Mercy: Demonstrates God's love and compassion by responding to hurt.

Ministry Gifts

Ministry gifts are the tools that God uses to build up the church.

They are practical, essential, can-do types of gifts such as those described in Ephesians 4:11-13. Many times, they are the people singled out for church leadership positions and ministry leaders.

Manifestation Gifts

Manifestation gifts are supernatural demonstrations of the Holy Spirit's presence and power. The Spirit of God is the source of these gifts, and they are manifested for the benefit of others to bring God glory (1 Corinthians 12:4-11).

THE VALUE OF UNDERSTANDING SPIRITUAL GIFTS

Knowing that each Christian has gift sets that are unique, valuable, and needed in the Body of Christ gives believers purpose in God's kingdom.

1 Corinthians 12:17-25
If the whole body were an eye, where would the sense of hearing be? If the whole body were an ear, where would the sense of smell be? ¹⁸*But in fact God has arranged the parts in the body, every one of them just as He wants them to be.* ¹⁹*If they were all one part, where would the body be?* ²⁰*As it is, there are many parts, but one body.* ²¹*The eye cannot say to the hand, "I don't need you." And the head cannot say to the feet "I don't need you!"* ...²⁵*there should be no division in the body, but that its parts should have equal concern for each other.*

SPIRITUAL GIFTS EXIST TO BENEFIT THE WHOLE CHURCH

1 Corinthians 12:7
Now to each one the manifestation of the Spirit is given for the common good.

SPIRITUAL GIFTS ARE ALLOCATED BY GOD

The spiritual gifts are given by God's choice; we cannot choose our gifts. Because He is working within His master plan, His appointment of those gifts to an individual can also help to serve as a clue to the work He has called them to do. The converse is also true—a sense of calling can serve as a clue to the anticipation of the spiritual gifts He has given.

SPIRITUAL GIFTS ARE OFTEN MISUNDERSTOOD

- Spiritual gifts differ from natural talents and skills.

- Not only are we given different gifts, but we are also given different measures of those gifts.

- God will also give us passions and opportunities in addition to our strengths and spiritual gifts.

- We must be willing to serve outside of our area of gifting when the circumstances warrant.

- No list of spiritual gifts in the New Testament seems altogether complete and compiling all of the lists together still may not result in a complete list.

Spiritual Gifts Application Guide

THE SPIRITUAL GIFT OF ADMINISTRATION

The Gift of Administration is the divine strength or ability to give direction and make decisions on behalf of others that result in efficient operation and accomplishment of goals. Administration includes the ability to organize people, things, information, finances, etc.

People with the Gift of Administration are strong on detail. They know how to take the pertinent details of a situation, and in light of the mission, put a plan on paper and start delegating responsibility.

(Luke 14:28-30; Acts 6:1-7; 1 Corinthians 12:28)

Do You Have This Gift?
- Do things like efficiency and promptness matter more to you than to most people?
- Do you get agitated when things seem poorly organized and you want to fix them?
- Can you bring order out of chaos?
- Do you naturally organize your life, schedule, finances, priorities, etc.?
- Do you naturally focus on the best possible utilization of available resources?
- Do you like to make decisions about *what should be done* and *when it should be done*?
- Do you enjoy formulating plans, framing policies and setting objectives?

Potential Ways to Use This Gift
- Chairperson or Member of a planning team
- Teams coordinator
- Volunteer coordinator

- Event organizer
- Administrative assistant
- Data management

THE SPIRITUAL GIFT OF DISCERNMENT

The Gift of Discernment is the God-given ability to quickly and clearly recognize and distinguish between the influence of God, Satan, the world, and the flesh in a given situation. People with the Gift of Discernment recognize what is genuine from what is pretense, what is counterfeit from what is real.

(Matthew 16:21-23; Acts 5:1-11, 16:16-18; 1 Corinthians 12:10; 1 John 4:1-6)

Do You Have This Gift?
- Do you feel a special responsibility to protect the truth of God's Word by exposing error?
- Do you often make a swift evaluation of someone or something that was said, that others did not see but yet proved to be correct?
- Do you perceive deception in others and it later proves to be correct?
- Do you recognize inconsistencies between words and actions?
- Are you mindful of moral sin and doctrinal heresy?
- Can you quickly detect any false teaching while listening to a speaker or reading a book?
- Are you sensitive to demonic presence and able to help people be free from demons?

Potential Ways to Use This Gift
- Member of a decision-making team
- Church officer or board of Elders member
- Member of a Counseling ministry
- Consultant to those who make ministry decisions

Week 7: Embracing Your Spiritual Gifts

THE SPIRITUAL GIFT OF EVANGELISM

The Gift of Evangelism is the divine strength or ability to help non-Christians take the necessary steps to become Christ followers.

People with the Gift of Evangelism care passionately about lost people and want to help them know Jesus. They are driven to understand the questions and doubts of lost people so that they can provide compelling answers. A person with this gift often prefers being with people in the culture, or even outside of the culture, rather than hanging out with Christians in the church.

(Acts 8:5-6, 8:26-40, 14:21, 21:8; Ephesians 4:11-14)

Do You Have This Gift?
- Do you find it natural to direct a conversation toward the topic of Jesus Christ?
- Do you enjoy being with non-Christians and sharing the gospel?
- Do you effectively communicate to non-Christians in a language they can understand?
- Does it bring you deep joy when a person crosses the line of faith?
- Do you like to equip others to share their faith?
- Do you find yourself being burdened for the spiritual condition of those of another culture?

Potential Ways to Use This Gift
- Local outreach events
- Mission trips
- Local ministries to immigrants or other resident nationalities
- Personal faith-sharing in conversational settings

THE SPIRITUAL GIFT OF ENCOURAGEMENT

The Gift of Encouragement is the divine strength or ability to encourage others by conversation, with written notes, and through acts of service and kindness. Encouragers are people oriented, discipleship oriented, and growth oriented. The person with this gift can usually recognize the potential of another person and can envision his or her spiritual achievement. Encouragers are process oriented and understand the steps necessary for people to apply truth and make progress in their spiritual maturity.

People with the Gift of Encouragement have an unusual sensitivity to those who are discouraged or struggling. These people also tend to have a high capacity of patience and optimism.

(Acts 14:22; Romans 12:8; 1 Timothy 4:13; Hebrews 10:24-25)

Do You Have This Gift?
- Do you love to see others mature in their faith?
- Do you desire for others to discover their Spiritual DNA and leverage their resources to live in alignment with their calling?
- Are you conscious of your example because you want to be a model for others?
- Do people who are struggling seek you out for advice and encouragement?
- Are you naturally mindful of those who are suffering and struggling?
- Do you enjoy walking with someone through difficulties, because you believe they can grow through suffering?
- Are you especially patient with people?

Potential Ways to Use This Gift
- Join the discipling teams of your church
- Offer yourself to make early contact with new believers
- Join a team that helps people discover their Spiritual DNA and find opportunities to use their capacities
- Ask for believers who are struggling with long term challenges
- Make yourself available to visit or make phone calls to the

Week 7: Embracing Your Spiritual Gifts

sick or elderly who are home-bound or in residential care

- Join the prayer ministry

- Ask pastoral care for a card-writing role for those struggling, suffering loss, or celebrating milestones

- Join volunteer appreciation events or teams

THE SPIRITUAL GIFT OF FAITH

The Gift of Faith is the ability to envision what needs to be done and to trust God to accomplish the seemingly impossible. The person with the gift of faith is enabled to act on God's promises with extraordinary confidence and an unwavering belief in God's ability to fulfill His promises.

People with the Gift of Faith trust God in tough circumstances when others are ready to give up. These people are often visionaries who dream big dreams, pray big prayers, and attempt big things for Jesus. These people tend to be optimistic, change-oriented, and future-focused. They believe the promises of God and inspire others to do the same.

(Acts 11:22-24; Romans 4:18-21; 1 Corinthians 12:9; Hebrews 11)

Do You Have This Gift?
- Do you view obstacles as opportunities and trust God for the impossible?

- Do you enjoy pointing others to examples of the power of God intervening in seemingly impossible circumstances?

- Do people who doubt the possibility of God performing the miraculous tick you off?

- When people have their backs against the wall, do they specifically want you praying for them?

- Do you maintain lists of prayer needs and the answers to prayers?

Potential Ways to Use This Gift
- Join organized prayer teams for public praying

- Join organized prayer teams for leadership team support
- Join organized prayer teams for specific needs of children, students, or adults
- Offer to be a personal prayer partner for specific leaders
- Join the discipleship team to teach the power of faith to new believers
- Offer written or public testimonies of Divine intervention to the communications team
- Tell your stories of God's power on social media
- Join the leadership teams of new start ministries
- Support mission outreaches

THE SPIRITUAL GIFT OF GIVING

The Gift of Giving is the ability to give money and other forms of wealth joyfully, wisely, and generously to meet the needs of others and help support ministries. People with this gift do not ask, "How much money do I need to give to God?" but rather "How much money do I need to live on?" with the intent of giving much of the rest away. The person with the gift of giving rejoices when he or she perceives that his or her giving is an answer to someone else's prayer.

People with the Gift of Giving genuinely view themselves as stewards and that every-thing belongs to God. It is not uncommon for this gift to be accompanied by the ability to produce wealth, though certainly not a requirement.

(Mark 12:41-44; Romans 12:8; 2 Corinthians 8:1-7, 9:2-7)

Do You Have This Gift?
- Do you tend to see the needs of others more than other people do?
- Do you see giving to a worthwhile project as an exciting honor and privilege?
- Do you give with a sense of investment and an anticipation

Week 7: Embracing Your Spiritual Gifts

of Kingdom ROI?

- Are you eager to motivate others to give?

- Do you intently look for ways to see a need met?

Potential Ways to Use This Gift

- Connect with under-resourced ministries to the poor and powerless

- Provide support for mission projects and missionaries

- Lead or help with fundraising projects

- Share testimonies of how God has provided for your needs

- Establish trust accounts and foundations to provide ongoing resources for ministry

THE SPIRITUAL GIFT OF HOSPITALITY

The Gift of Hospitality is the divine strength or ability to create warm, welcoming environments to welcome strangers and entertain guests in a home, an office, the church, or other gathering places. People with the Gift of Hospitality tend to have an "open home" where others are welcome to visit.

(Acts 16:14-15; Romans 12:13, 16:23; Hebrews 13:1-2; 1 Peter 4:9)

Do You Have This Gift?

- Do you enjoy having people in your home?

- Do you enjoy watching people interact in warm and inviting gatherings you help to plan and host?

- Did you choose or design your home with entertaining visitors in mind?

- Do most people feel comfortable to drop by and visit unannounced?

Potential Ways to Use This Gift

- Host a small group Bible study

- Offer your home as a meeting place for student ministries, or kids groups to meet

- Offer your home to leadership to be used for meetings or new attendees

THE SPIRITUAL GIFT OF INTERCESSION

The Gift of Intercession is the divine strength or ability to stand in the gap in prayer for someone, something, or someplace, believing for profound results. This gift is the special enablement that God gives to certain members of the Body of Christ to pray (especially on behalf of and for others) for extended periods of time on a regular basis and see frequent and specific answers to their prayers.

(Hebrews 7:25; Colossians 1:9-12; 4:12-13; James 5:14-16)

Do You Have This Gift?
- Do you see some of the issues in people's lives as challenges that can only be fully resolved through prayer?

- Do you set a daily time to pray for spiritual victories over the challenges and obstacles of others?

- Do you pray in response to a leading from God, whether understood or not?

- Do you believe that the work of Satan and the demonic can be resisted in the lives of people, ministries, and world circumstances through prayer?

- Do you find yourself unwilling to settle for the challenging circumstances in people's lives that look to be beyond the help of natural resolution?

Potential Ways to Use This Gift
- Join organized prayer teams for public praying

- Join organized prayer teams for leadership team support

- Join organized prayer teams for specific needs of children, students, or adults

- Offer to be a personal prayer partner for specific leaders

- Offer to be a prayer warrior with access to list of the needs of your church and its people

- Participate at some level in the National Day of Prayer

THE SPIRITUAL GIFT OF KNOWLEDGE

The Gift of Knowledge is the God-given ability to learn, understand, remember, and recount insights from the Bible, the experiences of their life, and personal revelations by the Holy Spirit. People with the Gift of Knowledge not only archive in their minds the truths they have learned, but are also particularly sensitive to the voice of the Holy Spirit to reveal facts that are not knowable by normal study about individual circumstances. They are supernaturally aware of how God's Word connects to every situation and how it informs every decision a Christian makes.

(Acts 5:1-22; 1 Corinthians 12:8; Colossians 2:2-3)

Do You Have This Gift?
- Do you love to study and research the Bible for insight, understanding, and truth?

- Do you have a good memory that retains insights from God's Word and life experiences?

- Do you sometimes get an intuitive sense that leads to "knowing" a detail or insight that is only explainable by a word from the Holy Spirit?

- Do people often come to you with difficult problems and questions, seeking your insight because they know the Holy Spirit can use you to give insights to them?

Potential Ways to Use This Gift
- Become a member of a decision-making team

- Offer your help in counseling or teaching

- Provide research for those who present biblical messages

THE SPIRITUAL GIFT OF LEADERSHIP

The Gift of Leadership is the God-given ability to recognize a clear and significant vision from God, and then cast that vision and influence to other people to harmoniously accomplish that vision for the purposes of God.

People with the Gift of Leadership tend to gravitate toward the "point position" in a ministry. Others tend to have trust and confidence in their abilities. They best serve others by leading them. They tend to operate with a strong sense of destiny.

(Romans 12:8; 1 Timothy 3:1-13, 5:17; Hebrews 13:17)

Do You Have This Gift?

- Do others tend to naturally want to know what you think and go where you go?

- Do you enjoy being the "final voice" or the one with the overall responsibility for the direction and success of a group or organization?

- When a difficult situation arises, do others look to you for input and leadership?

- Do you usually take leadership in a group where none exists?

- Do you find leadership enjoyable rather than frustrating and difficult?

- Do others look to you to make major decisions for a group or organization?

Potential Ways to Use This Gift

- Become a leader within your church team's ministry or a community service organization

- Become a leader of a small group

- Offer your gift to your church leadership team

THE SPIRITUAL GIFT OF MERCY

The Gift of Mercy is the capacity to feel and express unusual compassion and sympathy for those in difficult or crisis situations and provide them with the necessary help and support to see them through tough times.

People with the Gift of Mercy are typically good listeners. They

Week 7: Embracing Your Spiritual Gifts

easily experience the pain of others. They want to make a difference in the lives of hurting people without being judgmental.

(Matthew 9:35-36; Mark 9:41; Romans 12:8; 1 Thessalonians 5:14)

Do You Have This Gift?
- Do you find yourself being drawn to people who are needy, hurting, sick, dis-abled, or elderly?

- Do you often think of ways to help those who are suffering?

- Is it unavoidable for you to experience compassion towards people having person-al and emotional problems?

- Does helping the hurting energize you or depress you?

- Do you find yourself responding to people more out of compassion than judgment?

Potential Ways to Use This Gift
- Join a team that visits hospital patients and shut-ins

- Join a team that comes alongside of the homeless

- Offer your services to a food bank assistance program

- Get involved in recovery programs, prison ministry, or social justice causes

THE SPIRITUAL GIFT OF SHEPHERDING

The Gift of Pastoring/Shepherding is the divine strength or ability to assume long-term personal responsibility for the spiritual welfare of an individual or group of believers by nurturing and guiding them toward ongoing spiritual maturity. The person with a shepherd's heart has a love for people that compels them to meet with people to care for them and guide them with biblical instruction. People with this gift find great joy in seeing people mature in their faith and overcome besetting sin and discouragement.

(John 10:1-18; Ephesians 4:11-14; 1 Timothy 3:1-7; 1 Peter 5:1-3)

Do You Have This Gift?
- Do you have a deep love for people that compels you to care for them?

- Do you enjoy meeting with people to listen to their life story and provide them biblical insights?

- When you hear that someone is hurting, is your first instinct to try to be of help?

- Are you able to point out sin in someone's life in a loving way that they receive as helpful?

- Do you enjoy discipling newer believers?

Potential Ways to Use This Gift
- Become a small group leader

- Join the children's ministry or student ministry

- Join community service ministries that come alongside of those in need.

- Look for groups where people are gathering with specific needs

THE SPIRITUAL GIFT OF SERVING/HELPING

The Gift of Serving/Helping is the God-given ability to joyfully work alongside another and help that person complete the task God has given them. A person with this gift serves most satisfactorily by doing tangible work. They are the precious, irreplaceable utility members of a strong team. People with this gift prefer to work behind the scenes. They also tend to find joy in helping alleviate the burdens and responsibilities of others. This gift is usually accompanied with an attitude of humility and sacrifice, as well as an ability to perceive the needs of others. Availability is one of the server's strongest character qualities. A person with this gift almost never says no when asked to help others.

People with the Gift of Serving/Helping tend to demonstrate a servant attitude, loyalty, attention to detail, and responsiveness to the initiatives of others. They function well in positions of detail and assistant leadership.

(Acts 6:1-6, 9:36; Romans 12:7, 16:1-2; 1 Corinthians 12:28; 1 Timothy 1:16-18; Titus 3:14)

Do You Have This Gift?
- Do you enjoy helping others become more effective in their work?

- Do you enjoy, maybe even prefer, short-term tasks?

- Do you prefer to work behind the scenes?

- When someone is doing a job poorly, is your first instinct to help them instead of criticize?

- Do you prefer to work in a supportive rather than a leadership capacity?

- When you hear of someone with needs, do you offer your services if possible?

Potential Ways to Use This Gift
- Make yourself available to SOS (emergency fill-ins) needs for weekend services

- Join the events team for setup and teardown

- Look for church and community service projects

- Join the guest service team

- Become an office assistant

- Join the grounds or maintenance team

THE SPIRITUAL GIFT OF TEACHING

The Gift of Teaching is the divine ability and desire to study and learn from God's Word and make the Truth clear with accuracy and simplicity.

People with the Gift of Teaching enjoy learning, researching, communicating, and illustrating the truth of Scripture. These people enjoy studying and learning new information, and find great joy in sharing it with others. The spiritually gifted teacher has great adaptability as to the format, which can vary from one-on-one discipleship to formal classes, informal Bible studies, large groups, and preaching. The spiritually gifted teacher will usually become a teacher of teachers.

(Acts 18:24-28, 20:20-21; 1 Corinthians 12:28; Ephesians 4:11-14)

Do You Have This Gift?
- Do you enjoy studying and researching?
- Do you enjoy sharing biblical truth with others?
- Do others come to you for insight into Scripture?
- When you teach, do people "get it?"
- When you see someone confused in their understanding of the Bible do you feel a responsibility to speak to them about it?
- Do you enjoy speaking to various sized groups about biblical issues for which you have strong convictions?

Potential Ways to Use This Gift
- Become a Bible teacher to children, students, or adults
- Become a teaching coach, teaching other teachers
- Make yourself available for input to the congregational teaching team
- Join a teaching team at the congregational level
- Become a teacher's assistant
- Become a tutor to children, students, or adults (cultural or cross-cultural)

Week 7: Embracing Your Spiritual Gifts

ADDITIONAL NOTES ON SPIRITUAL GIFTS:

Week 8: ReCalculating the Value of Relationships and Your Own Worth

WELCOME AND OPENING PRAYER

God has always used people as junior partners in His development and guidance for His people. Different individuals play different roles. They use a combination of their spiritual gifts as well as the position or relationship they have been given or you have entrusted to them.

PEOPLE
Those who have spoken into your life and those who are speaking into your life now

1 Timothy 4:12, 14
Don't let anyone look down on you because you are young, but set an example for the believers in speech, in life, in love, in faith, and in purity. ¹⁴Do not neglect your gift, which was given you through <u>a prophetic message</u> when the body of elders laid their hands on you.

2 Timothy 1:5-7
I have been reminded of your sincere faith, which first lived in your grandmother Lois and in your mother Eunice and, I am persuaded, now lives in you also. ⁶For this reason I remind you to fan into flame the gift of

> *God, which is in you through the laying on of my hands. ⁷For God did not give us a spirit of timidity, but a spirit of power, of love and of self-discipline.*

Identifying the God-Given Entourage for your Journey

We were never intended to travel alone in our walk to follow Christ. We really are better together. You can be sure that God has an entourage for you. Look at the people and their roles in Timothy's life. As we look at his God-given traveling companions, let God remind you of the people who have played similar roles in your life. If that list is thin, keep your eyes open and expect God to fill those roles in your life during this new season of opportunities.

In just these two passages in the letters Paul sent to Timothy, he identifies precious people in Timothy's life. The role of people is huge in God's development of our spiritual maturity.

Paul pens the classic passage of the powerful role of **family** in the formation of our Faith. Timothy's grandmother and mother were his **role models of faith**. People who play that role not only model, but they are also intentional about instilling the principles of faith in our thinking. Those relationships should be cherished and celebrated as you live out your calling. Those relationships should serve as models in your roles to the next generations of your family.

Paul states that Timothy had **God-friends** — people who prayed for him with the awareness that God had plans for him. They believed in him. They prayed strategically and fervently for him.

Paul, himself, plays the role of an **accountability partner** to Timothy. Paul knew Timothy's calling, his personality — both, strengths and vulnerabilities — and the God-moments he had experienced. Paul reminded him of the milestones he had experienced, and exhorted him to follow through with the calling God had assigned to him.

Paul also played the role of a **mentor**. With the intimate knowledge he had of Timothy, he invited him into opportunities to live out his calling with the gifts and strengths that God had given to him. They worked side-by-side, and they worked individually in different roles, yet for the same outcome — his maturity and effectiveness in his calling.

Remembering the God-Inspired Messages People Have Spoken

Paul is not talking about singing Kumbaya around the campfire in this passage. Paul wanted to take Timothy back to a tender moment when he *knew* he had heard from God. Paul didn't need to repeat everything that was said. All he needed to do was remind Timothy of the tender experience.

Paul chooses a Greek word in 4:14 that is here translated as a *prophetic message*. The word Paul uses signifies "the speaking forth of the mind and counsel of God." Timothy had heard from God through the voice of a trusted friend.

Remembering *what* was said to you in those precious "aha" experiences of life is as important as remembering *who* said them. The weight of *what* has been said is increased with the *depth* of your relationship with the person God used to speak them. We must always nurture the relationships God can use to speak a clarifying word to us in our lives.

TABLE TALK

- Who are the people that have played a role in your life that are comparable to those that Paul identifies in Timothy's life? Who has God used in the past to speak into your life?

- What impacts did they have and what were the messages they spoke to you?

- Who is speaking into your life *now* to guide and encourage you as you discover your calling?

RECALCULATING YOUR WORTH

We have talked about how we can begin to feel like a misfit in the very world we live in—out of place, out of step, or even off the radar with the people around us, almost like aliens in a foreign land. There is also a vulnerability to an even larger problem: What if, wherever we are, we've begun to discount ourselves?

> ***Psalms 19:1***
> *The heavens declare the **glory** of God; the skies proclaim the work of His hands.*
>
> ***2 Chronicles 7:1***
> *When Solomon finished praying, fire came down from heaven and consumed the burnt offering and the sacrifices, and the **glory** of the Lord filled the temple.*

The word "glory" is used when translating the Hebrew word "*kabod*" in the Bible. Curiously, *kabod* is derived from a root with the basic meaning of "heavy." From this root came, among other things, a word meaning "rich." Speakers of ancient Hebrew would refer to a rich person as "heavy in wealth," much as we might say someone is loaded. A similar extension of the literal sense of *kabod* included being loaded with power, reputation, or honor. It's from this use of the word that we get the meaning of glory. God's glory is God's weightiness in wonderful qualities such as might, beauty, goodness, justice, honor, and power.

- The Psalmist, David, points to the abundant evidence of the invisible God's "weightiness" displayed in Creation.

- 2 Chronicles uses the word *kabod* to refer to the awesome presence of God at the Temple dedication.

- In 1 Samuel 4, we see in it in the Story of Ichabod, where the heartbreaking outcry is that the glory (*kabod*) has departed ("i" is a prefix for negation).

- The same word *kabod* is used to describe the weightiness, or worth, of Joseph as he had risen through the ranks of Egyptian leadership. He told his brothers to tell his father of his "glory," or *kabod*.

HOW IS YOUR *KABOD* THESE DAYS?
Are you feeling worth-less-ness or worth-i-ness?

The Bible records the story of Moses spending time alone with God during the writing of the Ten Commandments. Included in that epic story is the detail that God's glory, or *kabod*, rubbed off on Moses to the point that his body had a holy glow and his face was radiant when he came back down the mountain to rejoin the people.

Week 8: ReCalculating the Value of Relationships and Your Own Worth

But Paul uses the story in a stunning, yet practical way. He says that as time passed after Moses' encounter with the glory of God, the holy glow began a process of fading. Moses is so embarrassed by the gradually disappearing radiance that his people put a veil over him to hide his diminishing glow of glory, or *kabod*. Fearful that the glory of God had departed him, he began to doubt his abilities. Moses was concerned that he might become less impressive among the people he was trying to lead.

 Coins represent the principle of *"kabod"* (*weighty and worth-less*)

Until the mid-20th century, coins were often made of silver or gold, which were quite soft and prone to wear. This meant coins naturally got lighter (and thus less valuable) as they aged. Vendors didn't care what the mint markings were, or whose image was imprinted on the face. They just cared that a $5 gold coin had $5 worth of gold in it. They would weigh the coins to make sure they weren't getting "shortchanged!"

Over the years and the wear and tear of life, we can find ourselves being worn down or nicked-up. We can see ourselves, or create a perception with others, to be damaged goods. Like a worn nickel we can feel like we've become a light-weight—perhaps even worth *less* because of harsh experiences and the wear and tear of life.

AN EXAMPLE OF RESTORING YOUR SENSE OF WORTH

This creates a huge issue that **must** be addressed. If we feel worth *less*, then what is our remedy? Isaiah is a perfect example of a person who was awed by God, but felt that his surroundings in life, the events he had experienced, and the personal choices he had already made had *ruined* him.

Isaiah 6:1-8
In the year that King Uzziah died, I saw the Lord seated on a throne, high and exalted, and the train of His robe filled the temple. ²Above Him were seraphs, each with six wings: With two wings they covered their faces, with two they covered their feet, and with two they were flying. ³And they were calling to one another: "Holy, holy, holy is the Lord Almighty; the whole earth is full of His glory." ⁴At the sound of their voices the doorposts and thresholds shook and the temple was filled with smoke. ⁵"Woe to me!" I cried. "I am ruined! For I am a man of unclean lips, and I live among a people of unclean lips, and my eyes have seen the King, the Lord Almighty." ⁶Then one of the seraphs flew to me with a live coal in his hand, which he had taken with tongs from the altar. ⁷With it he touched my mouth and said, "See, this has touched your lips; your guilt is taken away and your sin atoned for." ⁸Then I heard the voice of the Lord saying, "Whom shall I send? And who will go for us?" And I said, "Here am I. Send me!"

Isaiah was awed by the overwhelming beauty and majesty of God—the Creator and King of Creation. But as he considered the worthiness of God while the angels worshiped, he became acutely aware of his own failures. He was overwhelmed with a sense of shame—his own personal worth-*less*-ness. What happened to Isaiah in this moment gives hope to those of us who have felt like we have lost our *kabod*!

God wants to address our sense of personal defacing/worth-*less*-ness. When we feel worn out, defaced, or lightweight, God desires to restore us to our full **worth-i-ness**. So often, that happens in personal worship and confession. There is never a better environment than in worship to expect God to point out Earth's need, share His desire to rescue, and respond to your willingness to understand your call. Our goal is to get to the point that we realize our *kabod* has been restored, and that, like Isaiah, we excitedly and passionately wave our hand in the air, shouting, "Send Me! Send Me!"

Week 8: ReCalculating the Value of Relationships and Your Own Worth

 TABLE TALK

Hard experiences, unwelcomed chaos, life transitions, and growing older result in feelings that you're losing *kabod*! Spend some time and share about the circles of life where you feel worth a little less than you once did.

HOMEWORK

- Complete the **People Worksheet** (p. 111).
- Spend some time prayerfully reflecting on your **People Worksheet** and the **Journey Map** (p. 107). Ask the Holy Spirit to identify those who have spoken or those who are speaking into your life, and most notably, what they have said, that may help you know the hope of your calling.
- Enter the names of the most influential people in your life and what they said or modeled in the People box of your *Calling Star*.

CLOSING PRAYER

Week 9: Gauging Your Resources of Time and Talents

WELCOME AND OPENING PRAYER

GROUP DISCUSSION
*'Aha' from homework: **People Worksheet** (p. 111) learning*

RESOURCES
A source of supply that can be drawn upon in order to achieve a desired outcome

No Discovery process can be complete when searching for God's calling for your life without due diligence to consideration of the personal resources of your **Time** and **Skills**. People stumble at the door of opportunity when they make uninformed decisions about their availability. Identifying your skills can be like putting on prescription glasses when looking at opportunities to serve.

Your commitment to monitoring your **Time** and leveraging your **Skills** can suffer from drift, distraction, and even detours. Both shed light on the pathway that leads to finding your current stage assignments and opportunities to serve in alignment with your calling. Gauging your **Time** and **Skills** as the **Resources** you bring to the equation can add powerful lumens to your *Calling Star*.

TIME: THE 168 HOURS AVAILABLE TO YOU EACH WEEK AND HOW YOU USE THEM

Every day is a gift from the Father of Life. How many days you have is on God. How those days are spent is on you. Time is a factor in your serving equation and must be put on the table when sincerely looking at where God is calling you to serve.

> *"The bad news is time flies. The good news is you're the pilot."*
>
> Michael Altshuler

God has blessed each one of us with a complex love/hate relationship with **Time**. Especially as a 3rd Stager, you are faced with a simple (but not easy) question, "Where are you devoting your time and energy?"

Psalms 90:10-12
As for the days of our life, they contain seventy years, or if due to strength, eighty years, yet their pride is but labor and sorrow; For soon it is gone and we fly away. 11Who understands the power of Your anger and Your fury, according to the fear that is due You? 12So teach us to number our days, that we may present to You a heart of wisdom. (NASU)

These are the words of an exemplary 3rd Stager: Moses, the stage in which you might be living, or one towards which you are heading. Moses was fully engaged in his Preparing years as a 1st Stager and his Building years as a 2nd Stager. He is most celebrated in what was an obvious 3rd season of his life. There, he applied what he had been prepared for in the first third of his life and now, investing what he had built in the second third of his life by leading the Children of Israel and helping them get to their Promised Land.

His life was robust, both as a boy and young man in the Egyptian palaces, and as a 2nd Stager; making a life on his own, discovering all the facets of his character, and preparing for the God-designed calling on his life after he left Egypt to lead his family and friends to the Promised Land.

In these three short verses, Moses acknowledges that even his own high profile, experience-packed life will come to an end and that he will experience what we all face – *the exit*. Not only does Moses address the seriousness of God's estimation of us and our response to Him, he then goes beyond, asking God to help him be keenly aware that he only has so many days to live. Moses teaches us to live each day with wisdom, no matter the number of our days, seeing life from God's point of view.

Psalms 90:10-12 teaches us at least three valuable lessons:

- Living like our days are numbered is not _____. (Teach us!)

- Making the most of those days is not _____. (So that we will yield hearts of wisdom.)

- We are _____ to God for how we live our days. (Gift to You.)

GETTING HONEST ABOUT YOUR TIME

Are you serious about discovering God's current assignments in the calling for your life? If so, it must include taking an *honest* look in the mirror to see how you are *really* spending your time. It takes asking the tough questions. It means examining your heart to make sure that your time is spent wisely doing what is important, meaningful, and purposeful to God's plan for you.

> "It's not enough to be busy, so are the ants. The question is, what are we busy about?"
>
> Henry David Thoreau

Acts 3 Discovery Participant Guide

Here is an example of the use of **Time** in a 168-hour week:

	Mon	Tue	Wed	Thur	Fri	Sat	Sun	Weekly Total
Rest/Sleep	6	6	6	6	8	8	6	46
Work	0	4	4	4	0	0	0	12
Leisure	3	2	2	2	6	6	4	25
Family	2	2	2	2	3	4	3	18
Mealtime	2	2	2	2	2	2	2	14
Personal Care	1	1	1	1	1	1	1	7
Maintenance/Chores	1	1	1	1	1	1	4	10
Wellness	1	0	1	0	1	0	0	3
Social World	1	1	1	1	2	2	2	10
Devotional Life	2	0.5	0.5	0.5	0	0	2	5.5
Serving	1	0	0	0	0	0	0	1
Travel	0	1	1	1	0	0	0	3
Unaccounted	4	3.5	2.5	3.5	0	0	0	13.5
Daily Total	24	24	24	24	24	24	24	168

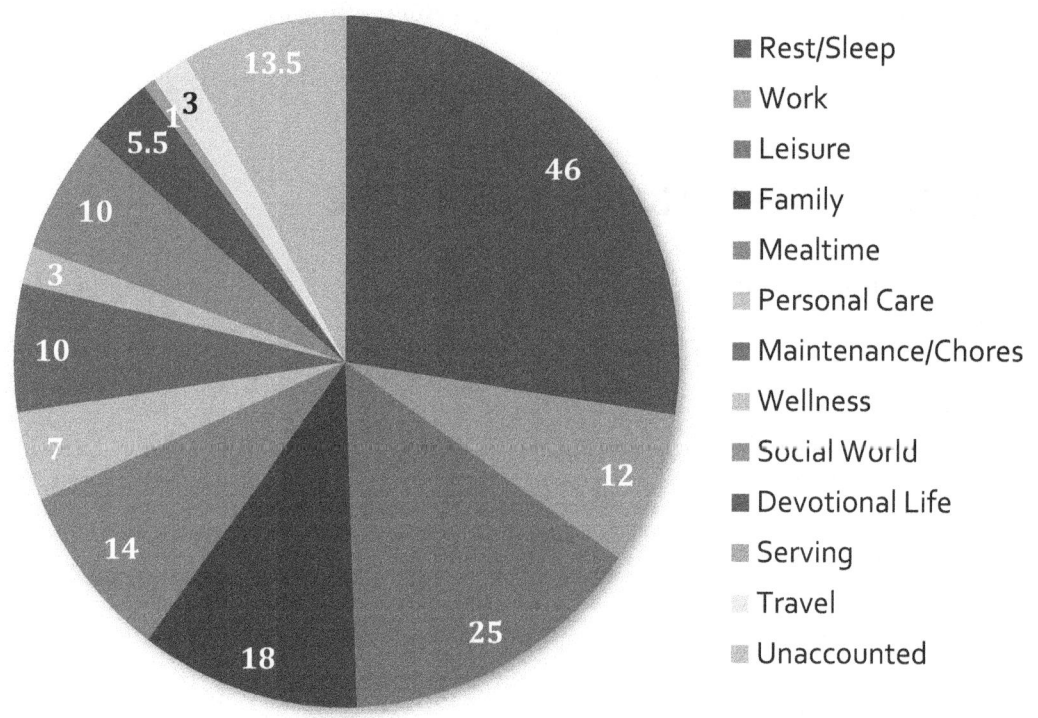

92

TIME CATEGORIES & DEFINITIONS

1. **Rest/Sleep:** Night time sleeping, naps, or general resting time that does *not* fit into other categories below
2. **Work**: Office hours, prep time (commute is under travel)
3. **Leisure**: Reading, hobbies, TV, or general 'alone' time recharging
4. **Family**: Nuclear family time, spouse time, dating time, support of child/grandchild, support, babysitting, aging parent care
5. **Mealtime**: Prep, eating, planning
6. **Personal Care**: Bathing, grooming, professional services
7. **Maintenance/Chores**: Household chores, shopping, property upkeep, personal finances
8. **Wellness**: Exercise, medical services
9. **Social World**: Friend time, social media
10. **Devotional Life**: Prayer, weekend worship, daily devotions, Bible studies
11. **Serving**: Church volunteerism, community volunteerism
12. **Travel/Commute**: Time spent traveling to/from places including work
13. **Unaccounted**: Remaining free time available

GROUP DISCUSSION

- What observations can you make from looking at this **Time** example?

- In general, how has your **Time** evolved over this season of your life compared to other periods in your life?

- Is there an area in your life that you anticipate is out of balance where you are spending either too much time or not enough? If so, what specifically is that?

SKILLS: THE ABILITY TO DO SOMETHING WELL; EXPERTISE

A cursory look at **Skills** may make them seem as something less than spiritual. Not true! The Bible is full of powerful examples of people with certain skills being used by God to win the day. David was both a musician and a warrior. A family in Israel carried the genetics, mixed with a tragic life experience, which equipped them to be the skilled songwriters and worship leaders of Israel. Arguably, the most powerful statement of the role of skills in God's plans is recorded in Exodus 31. Like us, God wanted to make the house.

Exodus 31:1-6
Then the Lord said to Moses, ²"See, I have chosen Bezalel... and I have filled him with the Spirit of God, with wisdom, with understanding, with knowledge and with all kinds of skills — ⁴to make artistic designs for work in gold, silver and bronze, ⁵to cut and set stones, to work in wood, and to engage in all kinds of crafts. ⁶Moreover, I have appointed Oholiab...to help him. Also I have given ability to all the skilled workers to make everything I have commanded you."

Skills are distinct from **Strengths** and **Spiritual Gifts**. Yet they are still beautiful expressions of God's handiwork in our lives that are inexorably linked with all our other attributes.

Kyle Parton, CEO of Epiphany Publishing says, "I see strengths and skills are different in that perhaps strengths are related to how I'm wired and who I am, where skills are related to what I do. They're different in that the former is internal and the latter is external.

Although they're different, I think they have more in common than they have in contrast. What they share is that they both need to somehow reference *action* to be meaningful at all. I cannot think of a personality or heart trait that is meaningful independent of action. 'Oh, her strength is that she's a caretaker.' That means she's skilled at assessing needs and finding ways to meet them. 'His strength is that he's a people person.' That means he's skilled at rapport building, networking, storytelling, etc. Both of those traits are made more real and concrete through action.

Think about the role of action in other common strengths. Even an abstract strength like creativity is only meaningful when describing what creative people can *do*. That is, what skills they have. They are

> *"It is possible to fly without motors, but not without knowledge and skill."*
>
> Wilbur Wright

skilled at envisioning original ideas, playfully connecting seemingly unrelated concepts, breaking out of common mental routines and patterns, brainstorming, etc. These descriptions are all built around *verbs*. Furthermore, if they don't have these skills, then I would argue that creativity isn't actually one of their strengths. So, my point is that **Strengths** and **Skills** are easily grouped by considering their dependent relationship to action. To depict it graphically…"

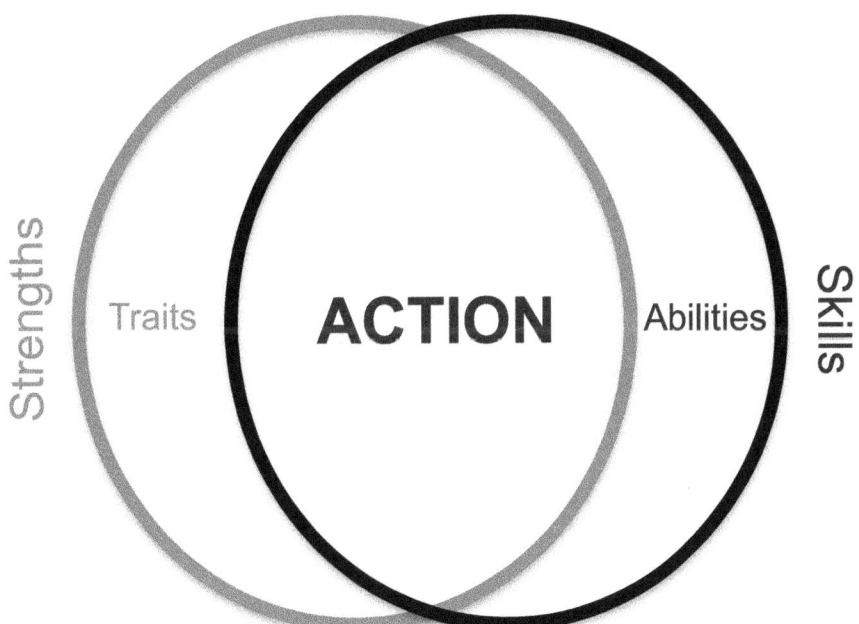

This entire Discovery experience is meant to lead to action in your next God-sized assignment in alignment with you calling. Do you believe Paul was right? He said, *For we are God's masterpiece. He has created us anew in Christ Jesus, so we can do the good things He planned for us long ago.* The Master Painter has blended the beauties of our **Skills** into the complete picture of *who* He has made us to **be**. And *who* He has made us to **be** is a huge indicator of *what* He has called us to **do**.

It would be incongruous to believe that God positioned us in life to develop **Skills** that He had no plans to use. So, take inventory of your **Skills**. Expect them to lead to action. And don't be surprised if the action nut doesn't fall far from the calling tree!

 HOMEWORK

- Complete the **Time Distribution Study**. Your facilitator will email you a link to an Excel-based pie chart.

- Complete the **Time Worksheet** (p. 117).

- Complete the **Skills Worksheet** (p. 115).

Week 10: Detecting the Heat of Your Passions

WELCOME AND OPENING PRAYER

 **GROUP DISCUSSION**
'Aha' from homework: Time Distribution Study

We've come to depend on the technology of GPS to get us from where we are to where we want to be, particularly when we're traveling in new land, or the route is complicated. Not only can it set our course to the desired destination, it can *recalculate* our course after we've made a wrong turn, or missed a right one. Sometimes we drift. Sometimes we encounter a detour. And sometimes we get careless or distracted. No matter the journey, course corrections are a part of travel and we must always find a way to get back on track. Whether it's the voice of the GPS or another person telling you to recalculate, there is something reassuring when you know there is a course correction in process.

For the final point on your *Calling Star*, we will consider in this session your **Passions**. Few points on your *Calling Star* will have more lumens to light the path to finding your purpose -- and the current assignments within that purpose -- than your **Passions**.

> *"If you can't figure out your purpose, figure out your passion. For your passion will lead you right into your purpose."*
>
> T.D. Jakes

PASSIONS
The good things that make your heart sing and the bad things that break your heart

FEELING THE HEAT

George Bernard Shaw was not a great role model for people of faith, but he was a great playwright. He was responsible for a quote that is worth repeating, if not all together adopting as a way to live your life. He stated, "I am of the opinion that my life belongs to the whole community and as long as I live, it is my privilege to do for it whatever I can. I want to be thoroughly used up when I die, for the harder I work the more I live."

Jesus did it before Shaw said it.

John 2:13-17
When it was almost time for the Jewish Passover, Jesus went up to Jerusalem. ¹⁴In the temple courts he found men selling cattle, sheep and doves, and others sitting at tables exchanging money. ¹⁵So he made a whip out of cords, and drove all from the temple area, both sheep and cattle; he scattered the coins of the money changers and overturned their tables. ¹⁶To those who sold doves he said, "Get these out of here! How dare you turn my Father's house into a market!" ¹⁷His disciples remembered that it is written: "Zeal for your house will consume me."

In this context, the word *zeal* means to be hot, fervent; it is the capacity or state of passionate commitment. We describe a passionate person as someone who is **on fire**.

Let's hit pause and do a quick remedial middle school science lesson. The Universe is made up of matter and energy. Matter is made up of atoms and molecules (groupings of atoms) and energy causes the atoms and molecules to always be in motion – either bumping into each other or vibrating back and forth. The motion of atoms and molecules creates a form of energy called heat. The more energy you introduce to the particles, the faster they move and the more frequently they bump into each other. The more frequently they bump into each other, the more heat they generate. *Whew!*

Week 10: Detecting the Heat of Your Passions

Now let's apply this kid's science lesson to what happens when God builds a fire in our belly. He stokes those fires in three basic steps:

- First, God gives us a new heart with the core values consistent with the Kingdom of God.

- Next, He infuses us with His supernatural power by giving us His Holy Spirit. When Jesus promised us that the Holy Spirit would come, He said that the Spirit would give us power. The Greek word we translate with the English *power* is *dunamis*. *Dunamis* is the word from which we derive our word *dynamite*. So, we're talking an infusion of supernatural energy into our souls.

- Lastly, He opens our eyes to the realities of the injustices and brokenness of our world.

The presence of Holy Spirit's power energizes our core values and they begin to smack into the heart-moving brokenness of the world around us. The bumping of our core values into the brokenness of the world around us causes a metaphorical heat—or fire—in the belly. The Greeks referred to that *"fire in the belly"* as **Passion**.

> *"The place God calls you is the place where your deep gladness and the world's deep hunger meet."*
>
> Frederick Buechner, American writer

The disciples recognized the presence and power of a personal passion in Jesus when He saw the abuses taking place in the Temple. They saw it was *eating Him alive*. Jesus couldn't stand the thought His Father's house was less than God intended; He couldn't live with those abuses He witnessed which dishonored His Father and hurt people. You are created in God's image. You are no exception to having the God-designed capacity to burn with a passion.

So, one of the ways God raises His voice to clarify His call in our lives is to build a fire in our belly, or give us **Passions**.

 **TABLE TALK**

Discuss the personal observations in completing your **Passions Worksheet** (p. 113).

- What did you learn about your gladness and your **Passion** from your reflections on what makes your heart sing?

- What did you learn about what breaks your heart?

- What surprised you?

RETHINKING YOUR FINISH LINE

2 Timothy 4:6-8
For I am already being poured out like a drink offering, and the time has come for my departure. ⁷I have fought the good fight, I have finished the race, I have kept the faith. ⁸Now there is in store for me the crown of righteousness, which the Lord, the righteous Judge, will award to me on that day - and not only to me, but also to all who have longed for His appearing.

The **Tour de France** is an annual multi-stage bicycle race, primarily held in France. The race consists of 21 segments (stages) over a 23-day period, covering around 2,200 miles. While the route changes each year, the format stays the same: the aggressive racing and risk-taking, the time trials, the passage through the mountain chains of the Pyrenees and the Alps, and the finish in Paris.

Paul had been living his own "Tour de Middle East/Europe," completing many pain-staking, miraculous segments in jaw-dropping fashion. He had traveled the known world. He carried the Gospel to Western civilization. He had completed multiple missionary journeys and established churches across two continents. He had written 12 books of the New Testament and was penning his last with the words we read. He had discipled a generation of people who had the reigns of spiritual leadership in their hands. His list of finished legs of his journey was long and impressive. Yet Paul's life-long journey had but one **finish line** in view.

TABLE TALK

- What are the main tasks of your current stage that you would describe as basically finished?

- What are the markers you'll use to confirm that you are truly finished with your current leg of your journey?

- What God-planned projects do you want to finish between here and your true finish line?

RETHINKING YOUR ULTIMATE ACCOUNTABILITY TO GOD

Analogous to our own judicial system with its many different courtrooms and their purposes, the Bible describes two distinctly different courtrooms in Heaven.

The first of the two courtrooms referenced in Heaven is noted by Paul in 2 Corinthians 5:10. It is called the Bema Seat and gives believers the opportunity to account for how they used the resources God entrusted to them. The second courtroom is referenced by John in Revelation 20:11. It is called the Great White Throne and calls unbelievers to account for their sin.

2 Corinthians 5:10
For we must all appear before the judgment seat of Christ, that each one may receive what is due him for the things done while in the body, whether good or bad.

Without the Light of Grace, reading this verse can send a shiver up the spine. How much more daunting does it get than the thought of standing before *the* Judge and having some form of DVR revealing a play-by-play account of our life on the Big Screen.

The two verses cited in this segment make it difficult for even the most contentious to argue the clarity of the statements. Like all of Scripture, you have to decide if it's true. But it's hard to debate the word *all*. And the word is used in both passages. The operative question is *which* all do these passages address?

As already noted, The Great White Throne scene described in Revelation 20:11 is a setting that is judicial and punitive. The *all* are those who are identified in verse 5 as *the rest of the dead*. This *all* stands in contrast to those in verse 6, described as *blessed*, and having previously participated in the *first resurrection*. As believers, we are part of the verse 6 crowd, making us one of the *all* of 2 Corinthians 5:10.

The context of 2 Corinthians 5:10 involves Paul's stated personal goal in verse 9 *to please Him* (Jesus). The purpose of the Bema Seat of Christ is celebratory and rewarding. This is the happy *High-Five-from-Jesus* atmosphere when He tells you "Well done" loudly enough that the rest of us get to hear it! Paul told the Corinthian believers that the thought motivated him to serve Christ. Then he used the thought to motivate his friends to serve Christ as well.

You can feel like the little boy who couldn't wait to get home and show mommy his perfect score on his spelling test. Acts 3 Discovery is designed to help you feel good about your spelling test and anticipate the moment you show Jesus!

> ### REFLECTION:
>
> *How would that courtroom scene go for you if it were to happen tomorrow? How would you like for it to go? What steps might you take to alter the proceedings?*

Week 10: Detecting the Heat of Your Passions

 **HOMEWORK**

- Spend some time prayerfully reflecting on your **Time Distribution Study** and your **Time Worksheet**. Ask the Holy Spirit to show you which areas He is calling you to focus on in this next season of life. Share those insights with a member of your church staff responsible for next steps in your discipleship walk. Use the insights provided by the study to complete the **Time Available to Serve** in the **Resources** point of your *Calling Star*.

- Spend some time prayerfully reflecting on the **Skills** you have developed through training and experience. Ask the Holy Spirit to make clear to you how He may want you to use your **Skills** moving forward. Use the insights provided by Him to complete the **Skills** contribution to the **Resources** point of your *Calling Star*.

- Complete your **Passions Worksheet** (p. 113) and spend some time prayerfully reflecting on your answers. Use the insights provided by the Holy Spirit to complete the **Passions** point of your *Calling Star*.

- Complete the **Next Steps Exploration Worksheet** (p. 121).

- Prepare to gather with your Cohort at a dinner setting within the next two weeks to share your Aha's and Next Steps resulting from your Acts 3 Discovery study.

Driving a Stake in the Ground

"The idiom, '(driving) a stake in the ground,' has its origins where someone would claim ownership, responsibility, or priority. For example, tent dwellers would put stakes in the ground to pitch their tents. Everything within the stakes was their land or home. Likewise, homesteaders would put stakes in the ground to mark off their newly claimed land." -Thom Rainer

Now is the time for you to "drive a stake in the ground" and claim the future and accept the assignments God has planned for this season of your life. We want to create opportunities for you to make your declarations.

There are three swings of the sledgehammer we want to help you take.

1st Swing

Get with one or two of your Cohort partners for whom you have prayed and with whom you have shared during this Acts 3 Discovery. Talk through your **Next Steps Exploration Worksheet** (p. 121) with them. Share with them the most strategic steps you plan to take, ask them to pray for you, and encourage them to check with you in the next thirty days on your progress.

2nd Swing

Even Heaven has planned a party after we all meet when this Age is over. So it seems very right for us to party together with your Cohort friends after completing this strategic activity designed to shed light on your new assignments in alignment with your calling.

Your facilitator will invite you to the place and time you will get together. It will be a time of food, fun, and sharing in the home of a host committed to your encouragement. Attend with your *Calling Star*, **Time Distribution Study**, and your **Next Steps Exploration Worksheet** in hand and be ready to share the most important insights of your Acts 3 Discovery Cohort.

3rd Swing

An Acts 3 Discovery coach will contact you or a time will be set for you to share with the assigned ministry leader of your church who will come alongside of you in your next steps of serving and spiritual growth. Provide for them a copy of your *Calling Star*, **Time Distribution Study**, and your **Next Steps Exploration Worksheet** (p. 121).

Journey Map Worksheet

Understanding who you are and how you came to be that way is one of the keys to successfully identifying God's Calling for your life and the evolving changes of assignments through the stages of life. Much of your behavior, preferences, and focus today are rooted in your past experiences and your response to them. Take some time to think back over the key experiences that shaped who you are as a person today. What were the major punctuation points, as well as the turning points?

Below are some ideas to consider to help you build your list of notable mile markers:

Life Transitions:

Education; marriage and family; career and employment; spiritual and religion; loss and grief; aging and retirement

Milestone Moments:

Jobs; promotions; achievements; marriage; birth of children

Important Choices:

Employment; relocations; relationships; personal values; health choices; finances

Seasons of Hardship:

Chaos; feeling stuck; times of uncertainty; pressures; scarcity; loneliness

Miraculous Interventions:

Lifesaving experience; family/personal miracle; near-death experience

Aha Moments:

Life calling; new life assignment; word from the Lord; timely insight; spiritual intimacy

Significant People:

Who they were/are; what they said; what they inspired

Traumatic Experience:

Loss of a child; loss of a pregnancy; infertility decisions; loss of a parent or sibling; broken home; marriage dissolution; catastrophic illness or accident

Your assignment is to draw your **Journey Map** in a way that tells the story of your life. Two examples have been provided for your reference, but remember, this is your journey, and it will be your story. It doesn't have to be pretty or perfectly organized; it just has to tell your story.

TIPS:

- We suggest that you may want to start by making a list of the experiences in your life to organize your thoughts before drawing.

- You may want to consider your life in seasons or decades to help organize what you would like to highlight.

- Try to set aside time every day this week to work on your life **Journey Map**. Ask God to bring events and people back to your remembrance.

- Feel free to highlight, color, draw pictures, etc. as God reveals those significant moments you might have overlooked or forgotten.

Strengths Worksheet

Reflect on the following questions and write down your responses. Next week we will spend some time sharing one-on-one, as well as sharing around your table, some of your responses to these challenging yet critical questions.

- What are some of your **Talents** that you recognize as **Strengths** that God has used in your life? What are ways in which you have invested in these **Talents** to grow them into **Strengths**?

- How have they been part of your **Journey** or played a role in the journey of others around you? Indicate these points on the map of your **Journey**.

- How might these **Talents** and **Strengths** play a role as you discover your calling and obey Him by serving?

*Pray and reflect on your **Talents** and **Strengths**. Ask God to show you which He intends to leverage as **Strengths** for your future as you serve in His Kingdom.*

*Write the top five talents on the **Strengths** part of your Calling Star.*

People Worksheet

Reflect on the following questions and write down your responses. Next week we will spend some time sharing one-on-one, as well as sharing around your table, some of your responses to these challenging yet critical questions.

- Who are the **People** that have played a role in your life that are comparable to those that Paul identifies in Timothy's life? Who has God used in the past to speak into your life?

- What was the impact of these **People** on your life?

- Have you ever sensed that God used someone to speak very specifically to you? What was the summary of the message(s)?

- Who is speaking into your life now that God can use to guide and encourage you as you discover your calling and obey Him by serving?

Passions Worksheet

Reflect on the following questions and write down your responses. Next week we will spend some time sharing one-on-one and as a group some of our responses to these challenging yet critical questions.

WHAT MAKES YOUR HEART SING?

- What gives you "deep gladness?" It could be a task, area, or impact you have experienced.

- What is so meaningful to you that you would do it for free?

- If time and money were no object, what would you do for God?

- Name *one* task you would stay up all night to complete. It is those passions you find yourself saying, "I lose all track of time when I am engaged in…"

- What activities make you want to get out of bed in the morning?

- What is something you will talk about to anyone who will listen?

WHAT BREAKS YOUR HEART?
Circle the below issues that break your heart

3rd world countries	Financial instability	Isolation	Single parents
Abuse	Health crisis	Lack of clean water	Veterans
Access to resources	Homelessness	Loneliness	Widows/Widowers
Addiction	Hunger	Mental illness	Other: _____
Disabilities	Illness	Poverty	
Elderly	Impoverished children	Prison/reentry	

What else breaks your heart?

If there was one problem in the world that you could fix today, it would be:

Pray and reflect on your **Passions**, asking God to show you which areas He is calling you to focus on in this next season of life.

Write your top 1 or 2 **Passions** (with notes) on your Calling Star.

Skills Worksheet

Reflect on the following questions and write down your responses. Next week we will spend some time sharing one-on-one, as well as sharing around your table, some of your responses to these challenging yet critical questions.

- What are some **Skills** you possess that have been instrumental in your **Journey** so far:

    o Professionally?

    o Personally?

    o Recreationally?

- What **Skills** are you hoping to continue (or start) to use as you serve in this next season of life?

- What type of role (or action) might you serve in various ministries using your **Skills**?

*Pray and reflect on your **Skills**. Ask God to show you how He has designed you to leverage these **Skills** to serve in His Kingdom.*

*Write your key 1-2 **Skills** or possible roles you might fill on the **Resources** part of your Calling Star. Be sure to leave room for **Time** (your serving commitment) there as well.*

Time Worksheet

Prayerfully reflect on the following questions and write down your responses. Please be ready to share some of your responses and learnings with your coach during your Coaching Conversation.

- What are the top three categories of life that dominate your time, such as family, work, chores, and leisure?

- What is the one thing you would like to do, but seem to have the most challenge with fitting it in? Why?

- How much time is God leading you to commit to living out your calling by serving?

- What changes do you intentionally need to make to fulfill your calling?

TIME DISTRIBUTION

The following table and chart will be provided to you electronically in an Excel document entitled "TIME DISTRIBUTION." We recommend completing this exercise in the Excel document.

- Reflect on the following categories of time as listed the Time Categories and Definitions on page 93.

- Fill in the estimated number of hours you typically spend each day in each category.

*Pray and reflect on your **Time**, asking God to show you how He is calling you to serve in this next season of life.*

*Write your new serving commitment (in hours per week) on the **Resources** part of your Calling Star. Be sure to leave room for **Skills** there as well.*

ADDITIONAL NOTES:

Next Steps Exploration Worksheet

One of the most important components of your Acts 3 Discovery Cohort is identifying and planning for your next steps in pursuing God's purpose for your life. This study was designed particularly to help you discover the connection between knowing more specifically your calling and serving His Kingdom accordingly in your next assignment. What new assignments does God have planned and you can initiate now?

> *"If God is your partner, make your plans BIG!"*
> — D.L. Moody
>
> *"Sympathy is no substitute for action"*
> — David Livingston

You may be still engaged with a career and family roles at a level in which you currently have very little time left to invest in additional serving opportunities. It still may be a perfect time to find weekend opportunities to serve at your church in ways more consistent with your *Calling Star*. It may also be a time to prepare for your future in serving, just as it is well-advised to plan for your retirement years financially.

The Holy Spirit may also be leading you to redirect your employment within your career, or look for a new career to align with how God has shaped you.

Your biggest discovery might be a rebalancing in the allocation of your time towards family roles and the spiritual formation of your soul.

While you may not have all of the answers just yet, our hope is that you can now begin to think through the following questions prayerfully and with greater insight and knowledge of yourself, your strengths, gifts, resources, and experiences that make you uniquely and wonderfully made.

Prayerfully reflect on each point of your *Calling Star*

- Which point(s) are shining brightest as you think about your next steps in this season of life?

- Is there a point that is still unclear to you? If so, go back to the worksheet for that point and identify the areas that are uncertain, unclear, or uncomfortable. Prayerfully reflect on the questions and your initial answers, asking God to show you what He wants you to know about this point of your *Calling Star* as it relates to your calling and next steps in pursuing it.

- Dare to dream. If time and money were no object, what would you do for God?

- How could you now combine your **Talents**, **Spiritual Gifts**, **Passions**, and **Resources** to take a step in following the path your *Calling Star* is revealing?

> *"This is our time on the history line of God. This is it. What will we do with the one deep exhale of God on this earth? For we are but a vapor and we have to make it count. We're on. Direct us, Lord, and get us on our feet."*
>
> Beth Moore

After you have reviewed your *Calling Star*, take some time to prayerfully complete the questions below. You will discuss your responses with your assigned coach following your last Discovery session. We also encourage you to be intentional in sharing with one of your new friends made during your Cohort. It is also a powerful tool to share with your group during a time set aside to celebrate with your entire Cohort.

- The most impactful thing that I learned or discovered by being part of this Acts 3 Discovery Cohort is:

- The points of my *Calling Star* that are the strongest drivers of my next steps and new assignments for this next season of life are:

- The specific serving commitment(s) and/or growth steps that I will explore, begin, or continue are:

Next Steps Exploration Worksheet

- The action(s) that I will take to begin to follow-through on exploring these opportunities and commitments are:

- What I still need to know/understand/decide to begin to pursue the next steps of God's calling in my life is:

- The resources/people who I will bring alongside to help me are:

About the Authors

JEFF & BECKY HARLOW

Jeff Harlow, with the unfailing support of his wife, Becky, pastored Crossroads Community Church in Kokomo, Indiana for 38 years. Their roles at Crossroads expanded from pastoring a handful of families to growing the church to over 3000 and reaching thousands across north central Indiana. As God prompted, Jeff led Crossroads through a successful succession plan, culminating with publishing his first book, *Dancing With Cinderella: Leading a Healthy Church Transition*.

Jeff is a visionary, strategic leader, driven to see things happen. Developing the concepts and tools of ACT3 Ministry was the perfect opportunity for him to use those strengths and leverage his experience as a 3rd Stager. Becky has been indispensable throughout the process, as her strengths of hospitality and flexibility have always been the oil for the multitasking team.

When Jeff and Becky transitioned from Crossroads, they reached a mutual agreement that whatever God had next, it must be done together—and God let them keep their word. This new season of life with ACT3 Ministry has yielded the sweetest experiences of all their time serving together.

Jeff and Becky still reside where they have lived for all of their 50 years of marriage. Their multigenerational family farm in Tipton County was the perfect place to raise their 5 kids and to stretch the limits of fun with their 13 grandkids. It's there that they live out the precepts of ACT3 Ministry and lead their peers in rediscovering their calling in this dynamic ministry.

About the Publisher

Epiphany Publishing, LLC is a private publishing company based in Indianapolis, IN. We are devoted to exploring catalysts for growth in the fields of religion, psychology, business, and human development.

Each year, Epiphany Publishing donates at least 25% of all its profits to nonprofit organizations that fight profound injustice—especially those atrocities that rob the innocent of their future. This includes the global sex trade, child soldiers forced to fight in war, and other forms of unthinkable oppression. We invite you to join us in partnering with luminous, restorative organizations like saribari.com, warchild.org, worldvision.org, and antislavery.org.

We are always interested in meeting new authors and reviewing promising manuscripts. If you've got a transformational message that you believe would be a good fit to publish with us, please introduce yourself at www.epiphanypublishing.us.

www.ingramcontent.com/pod-product-compliance
Lightning Source LLC
LaVergne TN
LVHW061342060426
835512LV00016B/2632